THROUGH
the STORM

A REAL STORY *of* FAME AND FAMILY *in a* TABLOID WORLD

LYNNE SPEARS

WITH

LORILEE CRAKER

THOMAS NELSON
Since 1798

NASHVILLE   DALLAS   MEXICO CITY   RIO DE JANEIRO   BEIJING

Published in Nashville, Tennessee, by Thomas Nelson. Thomas Nelson is a registered
trademark of Thomas Nelson, Inc.

Page design by Mandi Cofer.

Thomas Nelson, Inc., titles may be purchased in bulk for educational, business,
fund-raising, or sales promotional use. For information, please e-mail
SpecialMarkets@ThomasNelson.com.

ISBN 978-1-5955-5156-6
ISBN 978-1-5955-5207-5 (IE)

Printed in the United States of America
08 09 10 11 12 QW 6 5 4 3 2 1

To the most precious gifts of my life,
my children and grandchildren.

I hope this book will be my legacy to you and an inspiration
for you to know my true heart through this incredible journey.

contents

Introduction   ix

vii

Contents

introduction

If you're looking for parenting advice, you've opened the wrong book.

I sure don't know how the rumor got started that I was writing a book of mothering advice, but let's just put that to rest right now. This is also not a guide to being the best stage mom you can be, nor is it a juicy tell-all.

What *is* in these pages, then? It's really the story of one simple, Southern woman whose family got caught in a tornado called fame and who is still trying to sort through the debris scattered all over her life in the aftermath. It's who I am, warts and all, with some true confessions that took a long time to get up the nerve to discuss.

There's no dirt on my kids in these pages. There are, however, glimpses into our family's life together and maybe a few insights into the forces at work in our unique world. Most people have no idea how fame can warp the closest relationships in your life, or how big dreams can turn into bigger nightmares.

> MOST PEOPLE HAVE NO IDEA HOW FAME CAN WARP THE CLOSEST RELATIONSHIPS IN YOUR LIFE, OR HOW BIG DREAMS CAN TURN INTO BIGGER NIGHTMARES.

This book is a bit of a peek through the keyholes of our various doorways, a reality check for those who think the rich and famous have it made. Newspapers and magazines often don't go deep enough to get the truth, and that's what I am offering in these pages.

Why would anyone be interested in reading about me? As I said, basically, I am a straightforward, small-town woman, mother, and former schoolteacher. I'm not terribly exciting, truth be told. But my family has had an exceptional journey—really, a wild ride—and people think they know us from what they read. But they really don't know us at all. Part of the reason for this book is to tell my family's story, from a mother's point of view, based in a mother's love for her children. The way I see it, wouldn't it be better for me to sit in the driver's seat, telling the tale, than some tabloid for a change? It's not as if they have the whole story anyway. I think if you walk with me for a while, you'll get a different picture of the ups and downs in that wild ride. For example, when you're done with this book, you'll know that . . .

- I never let my teenage daughter and her boyfriend live together while she was under my roof;
- I have never been a manager for either of my girls—ever. And the only time I was ever on "the payroll" was when I was helping Britney with her fan club and Web site;
- and—surprise, surprise—I never "pushed" either of my daughters into show business. Nope, didn't happen.

Honestly, I'm not all that concerned about persuading people to think well of me or to change their minds about me. That's really the least of my motives for putting pen to paper here.

One reason I've written this book is to honor Mark Steverson, an entertainment lawyer who strategically planned Britney's career. He worked with Larry Rudolph, her manager, but somehow Mark never got the proper credit for all he did to help Britney along. Mark was a wonderful, kind man who always encouraged me to do something with the poems and the journal entries I had written over the years, but every time we were going to pursue a publishing project together, something would happen with one of my kids, and I got distracted. That fine man died in 2007, of cancer, and he never got to see this dream of ours come true.

The biggest reason I am writing this book, however, is tied to my relationship with my older sister, Sandra.

In the fall of 2006, Sandra was very ill with cancer, and she only had a few months left to live. As I watched her put the loose ends of her life in order, I saw how important it was for her to have all aspects of her life settled, not only for her peace of mind, but for her loved ones.

I took a good look at myself and realized that if God were to take me, I wanted my children to know what my thoughts were about the most important elements of this life. I wanted them to see me as a person, not just their mother, and share some of the ways I had gotten through my toughest times.

I wrote them a poem, a very amateur poem, but one that came from the heart. I had a friend write it out three times in calligraphy and then had each poem framed and gift wrapped for Bryan, Britney, and Jamie Lynn to open on Christmas Day.

I started with a little note:

Dear children,

We are never promised tomorrow, so I thought it would be wise to give you advice on life. I made my mistakes, and by drudging through them the best I knew how, I write this to you with a firm belief this is true. . . .

And then there is the poem itself, which deals with themes of choosing the right path, allowing God to lead them on their journeys, and being loyal to their faith, family, and friends. There are pieces of the poem in these pages, but most of it I will save for them alone. They have so few things that are private and sacred in their lives anymore.

This book is an outgrowth of that poem, the result of my wanting to hand something permanent down to my children and grandchildren, a record of our lives together and a record of their mother's love for them. It's to help them know me as a human being, as a woman and not just as their mother. It's written with the hope that when they see more of the real me, they will forgive me for any way I may have failed them, and I will keep trying to forgive myself.

The truth is, I never wanted this life.

It goes completely against the grain for me to go from one disaster to another—there is very little of the calm and peace that I crave these days, no middle ground, just a series of high highs and low lows. Most people write their memoirs after things have settled down a bit, and they are looking back at the crazy peaks and valleys from a more stable vantage point.

That did not happen in this case. After I signed on to write this book, everything spiraled downward into the lowest of the lows I had yet to experience. The curiosity people once had about my older daughter intensified into an unhealthy obsession shared by millions, and my younger child got caught in the buzz saw, her most private, personal matters becoming the subject of national controversy.

People always ask me how I get through all of it, how I manage to hold my head up in a world that judges me continually and severely.

This book will hopefully tell you how.

one

FROM THERE TO HERE

I remember one night in 2000, when Britney was on stage, wearing a beautiful, glittery costume and singing to the rafters of a packed-out arena. Thousands of lighters were flickering all over the room, held by music fans who were swaying and singing along to every lyric of every song.

Something about that scene reminded me, somehow, of the first time Britney was ever on any kind of a stage, as a shy little girl of four, with her head cocked to the side and her hands clasped. It was at the Christmas program of the day care I owned and operated, and she was singing "What Child Is This?" in her tiny angel voice.

How did we ever get from there to here?

Her dreams had come true, beyond her wildest imagination, and now she was up on this huge stage, sharing her gift with so many people. It was such a golden time. My

Golden Girl: Britney's first dance recital.

I

heart swelled with pride, not only for her, but for her siblings as well. Jamie Lynn was just nine years old, doing well in school and thriving with her social life with her friends. Bryan, my oldest, was in New York City, proving himself as a businessman, making new friends, and becoming the man I knew he could be.

My children's dreams were coming true, and so, in a way, were mine. My marriage had ended, and with it years of pain and shame. I was free of all that for the first time in twenty-four years, and it felt amazing. Britney was building me a big, beautiful home, prettier and more grandiose than anything I ever imagined I would have. The two of us had traveled to some fantastic, exotic locations and had such wonderful times together.

I was on top of the world.

And then things came tumbling down.

It's hard to believe things can change so drastically in seven short years. In January 2007, my sister died, and two weeks later, I got a call that would irrevocably change my life forever. The caller told me something so shocking, so disturbing, I could barely believe that it was true. But soon enough, I was to see the evidence with my own two eyes. I wanted to be in denial, but I couldn't deny the video footage unfolding in front of me. It was Britney, and she was shaving off her beautiful hair. All I could think of was, *How can this be? She used to be the happiest little girl in the world.*

To see that girl, with such despondency in her eyes . . . it broke my heart in a million pieces. My world was crumbling around me. And once again, I wondered, *How did we ever get from there to here?*

two

KENTWOOD

My sister, Sandra, did not have her official driver's license when we used to go driving together, she at the wheel and me riding shotgun, cracking gum and letting the wind blow through my hair. We were country girls, through and through. In those days in rural places it was common to have twelve-, thirteen-, and fourteen-year-olds tooling around back roads and even town streets in their daddies' cars.

When Sandra was about fifteen, Mama sent her to Kentwood to get some groceries, and as usual, I was her wing woman. Sandra was quite responsible and a good driver—for a fifteen-year-old!—but that day she hit another car, and not just any car either, a gleaming Cadillac with a boat hooked up to the back of it. Neither of us was hurt, but when Daddy found out, he was livid.

"You couldn't have hit a beat-up old Ford pickup, could you?" He stormed and sputtered. "Nooo. You had to go and hit a Cadillac with a boat hookup!"

Sandra was in the doghouse forever.

Daddy never forgot that wreck. Countless times before Sandra was about to step out the door and go someplace, he would throw in his two cents: "Sandra, be careful. Watch what you're doing. I don't want you to go hitting another Cadillac, now. You take care of yourself, because I don't want to lose you!"

With everything that happened in my life after I became an adult and a mother, I'm grateful my heart was not hardened to those beautiful times, although I doubt *beautiful* is the word my daddy would have used at the time. *Expensive* was more like it. Now that Sandra is gone, these memories bring healing and comfort, tears and laughter. I can still see her face when she hit that Cadillac!

When the hard moments and hours of grief threaten to overtake me, these snapshots from our lives together give me strength.

From Malta to Louisiana

Kentwood, Louisiana, is not exactly an exotic destination. There's basically the Kentwood Café, Connie's Jewelers, a bunch of dollar stores, and a Sonic Drive-In, the hub of the community. Everybody knows everybody for generations, and my daddy's people have been in that area as far back as anyone can remember.

But on my mama's side, the family tree is a little more colorful and glamorous. Her father, my grandfather, was Anthony Portelli, who came from the island of Malta. Malta is a small, densely populated nation consisting of seven islands in the Mediterranean Sea. It lies south of Sicily, east of Tunisia, and north of Libya, in case you were curious. Now you'll know the answer next time you're on a TV quiz show.

Anthony Portelli came to England in the 1920s, married a British girl, and changed his name to Portell. The Portells had two daughters: Joan, my aunt, and Lillian, my mother.

Mama grew up in London, a city she loved and missed until the day she died. I can remember her telling me stories of how she and her family survived the Blitz. In September 1940, the Nazis began their sustained bombing of the United Kingdom by blasting my mother's hometown for fifty-seven nights in a row.

She had a bit of a stubborn streak, and one night during the Blitz, she didn't want to go to the air raid shelter across the street from her house. It was a nasty, dirty, smelly place, she said, and she refused to join her parents and sister, despite their pleading with her to come. It wasn't a good night to test fate, as it turned out. The shelling was so close, the roof of their house was blown right off.

Mama grabbed her beloved dog and ran screaming across the street, with her father yelling, "Run, Lil, run!" She cut her feet running on the broken glass all over the ground, but she made it to the air raid shelter, safe and sound.

It must have been soon after that when my parents met. Daddy was in the United States Army, serving his country overseas during World War II. There were dances in London for the soldiers, and at one such dance, Barney Bridges and Lillian Portell first laid eyes on each other. Mama was lovely, with her father's dark Maltese coloring, and she just sparkled with fun. Daddy was very handsome, too, but he also had an advantage over the other American soldiers: as a driver for the U.S. generals, he had access to some goodies that must have seemed very appealing during the heavy rationing of the day. Essentially, he wooed my mother with candy and cheese, which was apparently effective, because she agreed to marry him.

In Kentwood, a local paper ran a photo of my mother, with her glossy, brown hair and her stylish London clothes. It was notable on the home front that a local dairyman was bringing home a foreign beauty from across the ocean. Thousands of young brides from Europe and Asia streamed into America after the war ended, but in rural Louisiana this was a bit of a first.

Some of those brides arrived on these shores pregnant, and their new

American husbands were no-shows. But Barney Bridges was waiting in New Orleans for his bride to fly in from New York City. He was eager to bring his Lillian home. Daddy had bragged to Mama about all the land his family owned, hundreds of acres of Louisiana soil, but as she was to discover in short order, a landowner in England is a far sight from a Southern farmer. There were no lush, manicured lawns in Tangipahoa Parrish, and there certainly was no genteel country estate. There were, however, dirt roads, snakes, and unrelenting heat.

The new Mrs. Lillian Bridges had some adjusting to do, starting immediately. Mama and Daddy drove more than an hour through dark, swampy terrain on their way home from the airport. "Where are all the lights?" she wondered out loud. A city girl to her core, Mama mourned the life she had in London, where she could walk down the street every day for fresh bread and produce. Southern cooking, on the other hand, mandates that everything—and I do mean *everything*—is fried within an inch of its life. She recalled with a shudder once how her in-laws would cook beans outside in a huge vat, adding chunks of lard by the slotted spoonful.

To Mama, she may as well have been a million miles from all that was comfortable and dear. She was homesick for her parents, her sister, and her country. The poor thing cried every night, and Daddy was at his wit's end trying to make her happy. Inside, she was always the fashionable London lady, yet outwardly she had to play the role of a farmer's wife, stuck in the sticks. But she made it. Mama was married, in love, and resilient, and eventually she was able to walk in step with the strange rhythms of life in her new surroundings. She even enjoyed some aspects of her rural existence, such as feeding the adorable calves. Of course, she always wore the most attractive Wellingtons—what the English call rubber boots—money could buy! Homesick or not, she was determined to make this new life work. And in 1947, she had another reason to sink her roots more deeply into American earth: my sister, Sandra, was born;

followed four years later by my brother, Barry; and then, after four more years, me, the baby of the family.

Years later, when I was in high school, our family traveled to England to visit relatives there. During that trip, I met Aunt Joan and Uncle Archie Woolmore for the first time and stayed at their lovely home. I think it was also the first time that I began to grasp just what my mama was missing so dearly on the other side of the ocean.

Mama as a beautiful war bride.

I remember being full of admiration of the British way of life. Sitting in the Woolmore garden, having tea with my relatives, I gathered that the English valued education and travel, and they felt travel was indeed an integral part of one's education.

Jamie Lynn and I in London, having coffee at tea time. We went overseas for the European Kids' Choice Awards.

Some of my mother's relatives were accomplished musicians, and one great-uncle owned a book-binding company. Engraved in my mind is how quaint and beautiful the great-uncle's garden was as we had tea amid his flowers and shrubbery. Years later, I would pattern the garden of my home based on my memory of that afternoon with the charming English book binder, my mother's uncle.

Someone to Watch Over Me

When Sandra was twelve, and I was just four, I would jump on her back and we would head down to the woods and this wonderful creek that was like something out of a Mark Twain novel. Well, maybe the creek was a little smaller and less grand than the Mississippi, but in my childhood imagination it was just as magnificent.

A picture of the three siblings at a family outing. I wasn't very happy (Sonny probably pinched me!)

We'd be joined by a dozen or so of our cousins, who were all more or less Sandra's age. They built rafts with hammers and nails, and I would help in my own little way. There was a huge tree with massive, gnarled limbs that bridged across the water, and we would climb all over it, back and forth. There were snakes everywhere, but Sandra kept a close eye out for them and a close watch on me. Until the day she died, Sandra was someone to watch over me.

Many of you may feel this way about your sisters, but I think that Sandra and I had a singular bond of closeness. One of my earliest memories is Sandra playing dolls with her friends; I was her living doll to dress and boss, and they had to make do with plain plastic dolls.

My big sister was so devoted she even brought me along on a number of her dates. She was a beautiful teenager with hazel eyes and a heart-melting smile, and she had her share of suitors, some of whom were none too pleased with having to share Sandra with the likes of me!

"I just want Lynne to come along with us tonight, that's all," I heard her plead in a whisper to one young man as I sat in the backseat of his car. Who knows, maybe she needed a chaperone on those nights, and I was certainly a less daunting guardian than Mama or Daddy would have been. But I truly think she just wanted me nearby, because we were two peas in a pod.

Family Matters

The dairy was a wonderful place to raise children. Daddy got up at 3:30 or 4:30 a.m. to milk the cows, and by 6:45 there was a big country breakfast on the table, with everyone sitting down to homemade biscuits, eggs, bacon, and cream from the top of the milk pail for coffee. There was no variation to this morning ritual.

In the summer we would run outside and build rafts for the creek and play in tree houses. There were moccasins and rattlesnakes galore, but do you think my parents ever told us to wear shoes? Huck Finn had nothing on us.

There were black widow spiders too. My Grandpa Bridges was bitten once, but I don't want to tell you where! Let's just say it's a piece of family lore that is best left to the imagination.

I loved riding horses. My favorite horse was called Wishbone, because my brother—whom we all call Sonny—wished on a turkey bone at Christmas for a horse. Sonny was just four years older than me, so he and I spent hours together, playing and riding Wishbone. After a good, hard day of play, we'd come in for supper and watch *The Andy Griffith Show* together.

Mama was the heartbeat of our home. It was immaculate, though we felt comfortable enough to put our feet up, so to speak. But the woman did vacuum every single day. We would tease her about her fastidiousness, because she even had a habit of clearing off the table before we were all finished eating.

"Oh, I'm sorry. I don't mean to rush you," she would say so sweetly in her British accent. "Can I get you something else?" She liked things to be pretty but orderly. Everything was in its place. When she was in housework mode, she could give the Energizer Bunny a run for his money.

My friends oohed and aahed at how she spoke and how pretty she was. Mama had thick, dark-brown hair, and she always kept it styled and lovely, no small feat for a fifties farmwife in rural Louisiana. I always wished I had picked up her elegant accent. She would laugh at me when I'd imitate her speech, and do you know she even had a ladylike laugh? My laugh is so awful it could peel paint.

One thing I did adopt from my mother was her love of books. Mama adored reading. History books, biographies, mysteries—she would check them out of the library a pile at a time. Like my mother, I often turn the pages late into the night. It helps me sleep, just as reading always soothed Mama at night too.

Daddy would rather visit with his fellow farmers than poke his nose in a book. He always wished he had a college education, but he had signed up for the army instead. All three of us kids attended college, Sandra for three years and Sonny and I for four. My brother and I both received bachelor's degrees—he in agriculture, and I in education—and in no small measure the credit goes to Daddy for gently pushing us toward college and instilling in us the value of learning.

Born Barnett Bridges, Daddy changed his name legally to Barney Oldfield Bridges, in honor of the race car driver and pioneer, Bern "Barney" Eli Oldfield, who died in 1946 and was the first man to drive a car at sixty miles per hour. In the thirties, when Daddy was coming of age, apparently there was a saying going around. If you were behind the wheel, zooming around like a speed demon, people had a comeback for you: "Who do you think you are, Barney Oldfield?"

"Daddy, do you know how silly that is?" I would tease him about appropriating his idol's name.

He would blush a little, look away, and smile. But secretly, he probably daydreamed about taking the corners at Daytona with a gleaming, souped-up Fiat or Blitzen Benz, just as his hero-namesake did.

We always had new cars, and Daddy loved to drive. He bragged about never having had a wreck and got such a kick out of telling stories about how his family—Mama, Sandra, Sonny, and me—wreaked havoc on the community by being let loose on the streets. When I play cars with my grandson Preston, who is obsessed with anything motorized, I like to think that boy got his zeal for automobiles from his great-grandfather, Barney O. Bridges.

We attended the Methodist church every Sunday—Mama and us kids would, that is. She had been raised in the Church of England, and she commented once that the Methodist church was the closest to the tradition she had grown up in, though now I can see they were not very close at all. Daddy would come with us once in a while, but he had some issues with "churchy" people. That's not to say he didn't believe. I would catch glimpses of him, lying crosswise across the bed, reading his Bible that was falling apart because it was studied so often.

He knew that book.

When spiritual gifts were being passed out, my daddy got discernment. He had an uncanny ability of knowing the true person inside anyone he was dealing with. This built-in radar in my father's soul meant he could make accurate predictions about a person's character, and thus what life would probably have in store for him.

One boy I dated did not meet with Daddy's approval. "You watch, Lynne," he said gravely. "That boy's going to run around on his wife someday." And that's exactly what ended up happening. Of another boy, Daddy predicted—correctly—that someday he would turn out to be feckless and live off his parents.

> JAMIE LYNN SEEMS TO HAVE INHERITED THIS GIFT OF SHREWDNESS FROM HER GRANDPA. SHE HAS ALWAYS BEEN ESPECIALLY GOOD AT SIZING PEOPLE UP FAST.

Jamie Lynn seems to have inherited this gift of shrewdness from her grandpa. She has always been especially good at sizing people up fast, almost instantly either taking to or just as easily disliking certain people. If she keeps it sharp, that gift will stand her in good stead the rest of her life.

Daddy also taught me to treat everyone the same, no matter their status, color, or beliefs. When I was a young girl, one of his employees was an old, uneducated man who had the tendency to hit the liquor pretty hard. Sometimes he wouldn't show up in the morning to help my father milk the hundred head of cows. Yet I can still remember how my daddy talked to this man, gently and with respect. Once I asked my father why he was so nice to this man. "The poor ol' guy has had a hard life," he said. "We don't know how lucky we are." Those words have left a lasting impression. I have always tried to teach my children to treat everyone with respect. Often you don't know a person's story, and if you did, you might very well understand his or her actions better.

Homesick

It's been three decades since Daddy died, and I am still longing for someone to take care of me the way he always did. All of these memories of Mama and Daddy make them feel closer somehow, yet I miss them both more keenly than usual too. My love for them is still immediate and strong, even though death has separated us for many years. Just as my mother remained homesick her entire adult life for England and her family there, I am homesick for my parents, for that safe place of comfort and security they provided.

I guess that will never change.

The way I was raised, there was a time and a place for everything, and our lives unfolded in a predictable fashion. The chaos that was to come in my own family life as an adult was nothing I could have ever imagined—or wanted. Yet in Barney and Lillian Bridges' home, I learned this: when you're a family, you stick together as a family, no matter what. That foundational truth of my life would be rocked to the core in the years ahead.

three

GOOD-LOOKING SOUTHERN MAN

In my era, people married young.

These days, people in their early twenties are considered almost too young to make that lifelong commitment, especially if they have school to finish, or a job to advance themselves in, or even travels to take.

But in the midseventies, no one blinked an eye at a young girl of twenty, with a year of college to finish, becoming engaged to be married.

People did, however, blink an eye at the fact that my fiancé had been married before, a brief union that was over almost before it began. Somehow, it didn't matter a whit to me that the man I loved had pledged his eternal commitment once before. *That was clearly a mistake, while this is the real thing,* I thought. Anyone can have a lapse in judgment and then learn from it, right? My groom and I would be going into marriage with eyes wide open.

I don't even remember meeting Jamie Spears. He was just a local boy who was always around, as far back as I can remember. Everyone in our small town talked about him because he excelled at basketball and football—he was the quintessential small-town jock hero, good-looking and popular, and he could have had his pick of girls in Kentwood.

I do recall seeing him at the town swimming pool from time to time growing up. He was three years older than me, though, so I'm sure he never paid me much mind.

After I graduated from high school at St. Mary of the Pines, an all-girl Catholic school, I was an education major at Southeastern Louisiana University, about forty-five minutes from Kentwood. One summer, after my third year, I decided to take it easy on myself and not attend summer school. On a sweltering hot Louisiana day, I ventured out to take a dip in the town pool, and who should be there, too, but the darling of local basketball fans? Jamie used to draw crowds when he was in high school, as people from all around our area would come and see this average-sized guy run circles around huge ballplayers; sometimes he scored fifty points a game!

That day Jamie and I got to talking, and soon enough his charms were having their desired effect. One thought buzzed around my brain as he talked: suddenly, the long, hot, boring summer that stretched ahead of me looked like it had possibilities. After all, there are few forces on this earth as magnetic as a good-looking Southern man intent on recommending himself to the object of his attraction!

By the end of that first little poolside chat, I had agreed to go see Elton John in concert with him in New Orleans. Of course, Elton John was and is my favorite singer, so Jamie lucked out with the timing of that concert. And we had a ball. At the end of the show, I was dying to go out with him again, even though I had gone into the evening still maintaining that I was not looking for a serious boyfriend.

What first drew me to Jamie was how fun he was. We had such a fantastic time together, and he could always make me laugh. He knew I loved to dance and would take me out dancing every night. My parents weren't crazy about him at first, which made it a little bit sticky, to say the least. They were not impressed that Jamie had been married before, and they seemed to think I could do better for myself. (What did they see from the vantage point of being long-married, mature parents that I could not for the life of me see?) But I fell head-over-heels in love anyway.

Jamie and I on our wedding day, with the justice of the peace.

My parents came around after we were married—after all, what could they do? My daddy especially warmed up to Jamie and ended up really liking him for his openness, friendliness, and good work ethic. Plus, it was obvious how much Jamie loved me. This doesn't mean, however, that it was smooth sailing getting past my parents' objections. What we did to get past those objections was something out of character for Mama and Daddy's third child, something they wouldn't have expected from a daughter who was usually compliant and obedient, at least about the major issues. We eloped!

Jamie was a welder by trade, and in those days he would take one-, two-, or three-month jobs at oil refineries all over the place. I was visiting him on such a job in Oswego, New York, when we decided to forgo the traditional Kentwood wedding ceremony—with white dress, flowers, church, and minister—and simply speak our vows on our own terms.

I did wear a white dress, a borrowed bridal gown from a friend, and

Jamie wore a handsome suit. But I didn't walk down any aisle to "Here Comes the Bride," with family and friends beaming in the pews, and my daddy didn't give me away. Instead, I gave myself away to Jamie as we spoke our tender, simple promises, to have and to hold, with a New York State justice of the peace officiating.

Beginnings

I got pregnant almost immediately after we were married, and my baby was born nine months after our marriage, which I knew would set tongues wagging in our small town. That's one of the things I used to worry about, that by God's grace I don't so much anymore: people's opinions. Little did I know that someday, everyone from little old ladies in grocery store checkouts to teenagers browsing online gossip blogs would have an opinion about me and my family!

Years later, when Britney got pregnant so soon after she and Kevin were married, I knew enough about marriage and kids and the combination of the two to worry that it was probably too soon for a baby. But at the time

> THAT'S ONE OF THE THINGS I USED TO WORRY ABOUT, THAT BY GOD'S GRACE I DON'T SO MUCH ANYMORE: PEOPLE'S OPINIONS.

when I was expecting my first baby, I so wanted to be a mother. I was ecstatic about Jamie, me, and the baby inside my womb becoming a family. School, I figured, would get finished one way or another. When I look back, I don't regret planning a baby so soon into our marriage, when I had more than a year left of college, but on the other hand, I didn't have a clue what was to come.

Our first year of marriage was really quite idyllic. We lived in Florida for a few months on one of Jamie's jobs, and we also built up a nice little nest egg. One highlight of that period was meeting my friend Jill, who has walked with me the longest and through more passages than any other friend. She is married to Ricky Prescott, Jamie's best friend, who worked with him for years at various construction jobs. Jill is like my stronger twin sister. For thirty-two years, I have called her to pick her brain on any matter whatsoever, to laugh with her, or to cry on her shoulder.

In hindsight, I truly fell in love with Jamie during our first year of marriage. Now, I loved him when we spoke our wedding vows, but I think what I felt then was more like infatuation, not a profound and abiding kind of love. Throughout that first year, though, our cup was full to the overflowing.

What I didn't know then was that I would draw on that reservoir many times in the years to come, until it was nearly empty.

four

CLOSE CALL

I was in love with my son the first moment I knew he was there, growing in my body.

Instantly, dreams of a little boy in pint-sized jeans and cowboy boots took root. Somehow, I knew he would be an adorable blond-haired tyke.

Jamie was so excited when I told him he was going to be a daddy, and he waited on me hand and foot. Ice cream, Snickers bars, fried chicken, hamburgers, pears and cottage cheese, frozen grapes—that was my list of nonnegotiable cravings, and Jamie dutifully drove to the store or fixed whatever I needed on that list as quickly as humanly possible.

Funny thing, I still crave ice cream with almost the same intensity!

We'd stay up late and talk about what our baby would be like and all the plans and dreams we had for our little one—what kind of house we'd have one day, with a big backyard in it for our child to play in, how magical Christmas would be with a baby, how we would get him or her involved in sports. Honestly, you could not ask for a more doting husband, and I was knit to Jamie, body, soul, and spirit.

My sister, Sandra, already had two boys, Rick and Todd. Rick had been diagnosed with autism around the age of two, which was so hard on Sandra and Reggie. Like Jamie and me, they had dreams for their firstborn son. Those dreams would have to be reshaped into new, hopeful imaginings for him. Just like every other child in our family, Rick is a gift to his parents and to us. Even back when he was a little boy, it was clear he was high functioning on the autism spectrum. Rick could take apart a machine and put it back together in a snap, and he still can.

My parents already had those two precious grandsons, and on April 19, 1977, they received a third, Bryan James Spears.

Tragedies

When he was born, Bryan had a pneumonic germ on his lung, which is another way of saying he had a bacterial lung infection. Because newborns have a compromised immune system, they don't have the capacity to fight an infection like that. The first night of his life, Bryan fought so hard, but we almost lost him. A first-time mom, I was terrified, vulnerable, and more invested in someone than I ever thought possible. It goes without saying that I did not leave his side. I remember pleading with God, incoherently and without ceasing, to hold Bryan's little life in his hands and to please, *please* give him back to me.

And he did.

Even after Bryan pulled through that first awful night, he was still in some danger. Any child that young with a significant infection is kept for a week or so, to make sure it doesn't turn into a life-threatening blood infection. I remember how frail he looked with an IV hooked up to his tiny body—it broke my heart. It also made me think of another mother losing her child.

When I was twenty-one and pregnant with Bryan, a piece of tractor equipment fell on my brother, Sonny, and I drove him to the emergency room as he was bleeding and moaning in pain. The roads were slick with rain, and as I was rounding the curve, an oncoming car was coming in the left lane. In a split second I could see two young boys riding their bikes on the road. In that flash of time, I had a sick sensation that I would hit one of them, that it would be impossible not to, as I knew my car would not stop, no matter how hard I slammed on the brakes. One boy managed to get his bike out of the way, but his friend, a twelve-year-old boy whose house was right by the scene of the accident, was hit.

When I got out of my car, he was covered in blood as I knelt down beside him. When the paramedics got there, they took him to the hospital, and Sonny and I continued on to the ER, numb with shock and horror. We must have gotten to the ER with Sonny around the same time as the boy's mother, who learned that her son was dead. I can still hear her blood-curdling screams. They will haunt me for the rest of my life.

> WE MUST HAVE GOTTEN TO THE ER WITH SONNY AROUND THE SAME TIME AS THE BOY'S MOTHER, WHO LEARNED THAT HER SON WAS DEAD. I CAN STILL HEAR HER BLOODCURDLING SCREAMS. THEY WILL HAUNT ME FOR THE REST OF MY LIFE.

God's providence permitted that boy's mother to lose her son, while I was allowed to keep mine, watching him grow into manhood. Why? I wish I knew. All I know is, I am so grateful Bryan didn't die during his first week of life, when it seemed likely that his tiny lungs would not triumph over the terrifying infection raging in them.

That incredibly intense baptism into motherhood has stayed with me to this day. The fierce feelings it brought to the surface were so potent they remain Technicolor brilliant some thirty years later. Bryan's close call affected me and affects me still, in ways I don't even fully understand. But I do think those horrible hours defined a piece of my motherhood, bonding us, maybe even more than a mother and baby bond under normal circumstances. All I know is that I've been protecting him ever since, called by God to watch over him, physically at first, and even now spiritually and emotionally.

Bryan will probably squirm when he reads this—what thirty-one-year-old man wants to hear that his mama is still protecting him? But every mother of grown children knows what I mean.

No matter how old your children are, they are still and always yours to protect in whatever ways you can.

five

WRECKING BALLS

I didn't notice Jamie's drinking problem until it hit me square between the eyes.

Jamie always enjoyed a beer here and there, but he didn't start drinking heavily until after Bryan was born.

He's just being a bad boy, I thought. *He'll eventually grow up.* That's the way I rationalized his getting drunk on the weekends.

It was a different time and place back then. In those days, when someone drank too much, you didn't automatically start thinking about rehab or even getting your loved one with the problem to join Alcoholics Anonymous. You just hoped that person would mature, or that a good heart-to-heart chat with your local pastor might do the trick.

This was my mind-set in the spring of 1978, just a little over two years after Jamie and I had pledged our undying commitment. In April of the previous year, we had brought our beautiful son home after a harrowing week of wondering if he would live or die, and we looked forward to starting our lives together as a family. Now Bryan was about to turn one.

Little did I know that two wrecking balls were on their way to crash through my perfect life: one, a tragedy that would instantly alter me for the rest of my life, and the other, an addiction that would eventually reduce my marriage and family to rubble.

"He's Gone"

Daddy loved his grandchildren so much. There were three grandsons then for him and Mama to dote on: Rick, age five; Todd, age three; and little Bryan, who was right at that impossibly cute, just-starting-to-walk, gummy-smile-with-two-front-teeth stage of a baby just about to graduate into toddlerhood. Daddy got such a kick out of those boys.

When Bryan was one week from his first birthday, he and I were at Mama and Daddy's house as we often were, just visiting with Mama and hanging out in the warmth and security of my childhood home. I can remember being in the bathroom and hearing my Uncle Dalton's voice in the front room. He told us that he had to tell us something.

"Barney's truck rolled over with him in it," my father's brother said, his face stony. "He's gone."

We were in a state of utter shock as Uncle Dalton gave us what details he could. Apparently, the man who had been with Daddy in the huge milk calibration truck said Daddy tried to jump out when he knew the truck was rolling over, and it crushed him. Those trucks are like tanks.

Daddy was gone. How could that be? It was the most horrific piece of news ever, unbelievable, shattering, and devastatingly true.

You are probably never ready to lose a parent, but at age twenty-two, with a baby and a husband who drank too much, I was completely overwhelmed.

A few days after we laid Daddy in the ground, it was Bryan's birthday. We decided Daddy would have wanted us to celebrate the occasion anyway, and goodness knows we needed to divert our attention from the grief we all felt. As if we could.

Mama wanted to have the party at her house, probably because she didn't feel like going anywhere else. Bless her heart, she was lost without Daddy. In her fifties when she was widowed, Mama never remarried; she went about her business living for us kids. She did what Daddy would have wanted her to do.

Sonny was just twenty-five, and he had to grow up fast and take over full responsibility for running the dairy.

So Bryan's birthday party would be at Mama's; it was settled—except for one problem: Jamie thought we should have it as *his* parents' house and would not be budged on the matter. He was positively irate that we would not change our minds. *Who cares whose house it's at?* I wanted to scream. If you've ever lost a loved one, you know that nothing much matters in the days and weeks and months of that fresh, raw grief. You're just trying to put one foot in front of the other and function the best you can.

Jamie disappeared for a week on a bender. No one knew where he was, and frankly—in my state of numbness and almost robotic condition of going through the motions of life—I didn't care.

If you have lived with an alcoholic, you can relate to the fact that Jamie had a way of creating drama at the very worst times. The very *worst* times, like my daddy's death. This is textbook alcoholic behavior. To say that I had little or no support from my husband at this time would be an understatement. At a time in my life when I was more hurting and vulnerable than I could bear, Jamie's absence—emotional and sometimes physical—compounded my loss, and I don't think I ever really grieved my daddy properly, to this day.

In our lives together, if someone was sick or even dying, Jamie would find a way to act up and direct everyone's attention to him. He especially drank a lot at any type of seasonal celebration; there was always something happening at Christmas, for example. One year he missed our family gift exchange around the tree. Try explaining where Daddy is when it's time to open presents and he's nowhere to be found, and watch the excitement and joy of Christmas fade from the eyes of the child you love. If you have tried it, you know your heart cracked wide open.

The Knot Loosens

After that, the unraveling of our family began in earnest. With every alcohol-soaked episode, our perfect little life began to unstitch, and the knot we had tied with our vows and our love started to work loose, thread by painful thread.

In September of that year, a few months after Daddy's death, I went back to college to finish my degree. Mama watched Bryan when I was at school, and often when I had to study. I could not have made it without her.

> WITH EVERY ALCOHOL-SOAKED EPISODE, OUR PERFECT LITTLE LIFE BEGAN TO UNSTITCH.

Jamie was not encouraging of my efforts, to say the least. Actually, in some ways he was actively working against me, undermining my confidence at every turn and making me feel—and sometimes believe—that I wasn't smart enough to hold a bachelor's degree. "You're too stupid to graduate," he would sneer. "How come they don't know that down at the school?" His words crushed my spirit.

It was a small miracle that I finished my college education and received my diploma in 1979. Really, anyone who achieves anything of importance while being married to an alcoholic is miraculous.

Two-year-old Bryan, my sister, and my mom sat in the audience and cheered me on that extraordinary day. We went out for Chinese food afterward and celebrated. No, Jamie wasn't there. He had to work.

I think one of the hardest aspects of my lonely achievement was that, at the end of the day, when I'd given all I had to give, there was no one there to hold me tight and say, "I'm so proud of you." Or I should say, the person I wanted and needed that affirmation from most wouldn't— or couldn't—give it to me.

At times when things were especially rough, Mama and my sister, Sandra, wanted me to leave Jamie. The one and only fight my sister and I ever had (it sounds crazy, but Sandra and I literally never argued) was after one of Jamie's benders. She got so mad that I wouldn't leave him.

When I look back, I guess I could have ended it a lot sooner and maybe saved myself and my son some heartache. But I wouldn't have my girls, Britney and Jamie Lynn. Plus, it's almost impossible to look back and say I should have done this or that. At the time, divorcing Jamie did not seem like the right thing to do, because for one thing, I didn't believe in divorce. I still don't. It bothers me when I see people, especially those with children, just throw away their marriages and not look back, or have no remorse whatsoever.

I loved Jamie, and I honestly thought if I loved him and stood by him until he grew out of his "bad boy" phase, we could live out our days together as a happy family. Plus, the man had the most amazing timing when it came to cleaning up his act—fast. Just when I thought I couldn't take another binge or another mean word, suddenly he would change his tune and transform into the ideal husband and father. Jamie kept saying he was going to quit drinking, and most of the time, I kept choosing to believe him, though deep down I knew better.

At times, we would have a blowout over his drinking or some woman I would hear about him flirting with at a bar. We would be estranged, and then I would take him back. I look back now and see that I was probably just as addicted to the problem as he was addicted to alcohol, but in the thick of it, all I could see was that I was married with a small child, and I had to make it work somehow.

When Bryan was about four years old, the threadbare patches of our dysfunctional marriage began to wear too thin. It was Christmas, and again Jamie found a way to point everyone's minds to him by getting smashed at his uncle's holiday party. When he was missing on Christmas morning, as Bryan and I waited by the tree for Daddy to come home and open presents with us, I was done.

I had enough of his drinking and disappearing, of his empty promises to quit, and of the roller-coaster highs and lows of our life together. I took Bryan and packed my bags for Mama's house, and for two weeks, I held firm: it was over.

We were separated, and I actually filed for divorce. That might have been the end of the little Spears family, right then and there. But Jamie got hold of himself, just in the nick of time. He did not want to lose Bryan and me.

Jamie's daddy and stepmother came over to Mama's and begged me to consider taking Jamie back. "He really wants to change this time," they pleaded. "He will do anything to get you back."

And he did, for a time.

six

SWEET AND BITTER

When you are twenty-six years old, it's easy to believe that love conquers all.

I certainly wanted to believe that Jamie would stick to his commitment and change his ways, and he genuinely seemed to be digging in deep to tunnel his way back to being a reliable and loving husband and father. First, he rededicated himself to God, and his renewed faith inspired him to work with the young people at Greenlaw Baptist Church, where we attended, and also to walk alongside some men he knew who were struggling with the same kinds of addictions that had brought Jamie to his knees. Finally, he replaced drinking with more positive activities, like working out at the gym. Jamie wanted so badly to be healthy in body and spirit.

His construction business started booming, and we decided to build a health spa together. This was in the early eighties, mind you, years before spas were to become popular. For our area especially, a spa was a novel enterprise altogether. The health and wellness aspects of the spa business seemed to spill over into our lives, and we both ate really well and exercised regularly. All the energy and attention Jamie had wasted on drinking he now poured into building his businesses, his body, and most important, his family. We were like the Barbie and Ken of Kentwood—it was that perfect. He became a devoted daddy, investing hours into his little sports nut's life as a volunteer coach for just about any sport you can name.

Life was so good.

When I took Jamie back, part of me was very skeptical despite my youthful optimism. Before I had decided to give him one more chance, I lost track of the occasions that Jamie promised me he would never stumble around our house or a bar somewhere, slurring his speech, acting like an ornery drunk, one more time. How many times had I heard that song and dance before? How many times had I been disappointed? So I didn't trust him immediately—it took almost a year before I really believed his turnabout was real. Day by sober day, as kind words replaced mean ones and destructive deeds were replaced by constructive ones, I could see that his actions matched his promises.

That time period, which I think of as our "golden years," was filled with friends and laughter too. We would throw these great big cookouts and crawfish boils out at our place, and we had so much fun. For those of you who did not grow up in the South, a crawfish boil is a seasonal, celebrated food favorite, especially in Louisiana. It's our version of a barbecue. We would invite a lot of friends and family, and we'd cook up some crawfish, or as some of us country folk call 'em, crawdads, in a huge kettle with potatoes, corn, spices, and herbs. Really, you could throw anything in there that doesn't cook to pieces! I have to hand it to Jamie, because he has the best recipe of all time for a crawfish boil—no one can touch him there.

After about a year of living peaceably together, we decided it was time for another baby.

A Baby Girl

Sandra burst into tears when she found out she was pregnant. She was thirty-five, had two lively boys that kept her running from morning till night, and another baby was the last thing she thought she needed. Of course, as I told Britney years later when she had an unplanned pregnancy, it's often those surprises that end up blessing us the most. That was certainly the case with Laura Lynne, Sandra's beloved, unexpected child and my precious niece.

I, on the other hand, was beside myself with joy when I found out I was carrying another child, whom I just knew would be a girl. We two sisters had opposite pregnancies in every way. Poor Sandra was scrawny and besieged by morning sickness, and I was the classic fat and happy mama-to-be, with energy to burn. We worked together daily at my daycare center, and every chance we got we would exchange tips, discoveries, and ideas about our pregnancies. Sandra and I plotted nursery details, swapped magazine articles on the latest and greatest trends in bringing up baby, and generally obsessed as pregnant women do about the new lives growing inside of us.

Mama worked with us at the day care, and she would chuckle at our little brooding hen parties. "You're wasting your time reading all those magazines, because when your babies come, you will just do what comes naturally," she would say, shaking her head. "Each baby is so different. You'll figure it out along the way. And if you don't, why, just call me!"

> BRITNEY JEAN SPEARS WAS BORN ON DECEMBER 2, 1981, AFTER TWENTY-ONE HOURS OF LABOR (BUT WHO'S COUNTING?). SHE WAS AND IS A BLESSING, GOD'S GIFT TO ME AND HER FATHER.

Britney Jean Spears was born on December 2, 1981, after twenty-one hours of labor (but who's counting?). She was and is a blessing, God's gift to me and her father.

When Britney and Laura Lynne were born, those girls were like twins from different families. As babies, we would lay them down for naps in the same crib, watching them sleep and marveling at them the way mothers do. Sandra and I would plan which Christmas gifts to get them, as we always got them the very same dolls or toys to open under the tree. Those two even wore matching outfits; that's how much like sisters they were.

Sandra and I shared some of the best moments of our sisterhood watching those girls develop a bond much like the one we had always had. I always liked to think about me and my sister and our little girls as being the four points of a square—sturdy and indestructible. Years later, Jamie Lynn would be in the middle, everyone's baby that we all shared and doted on.

The Sweet

When I look back on those five years of our life together, when Jamie and I were so close and we had two beautiful children, they were far and above finer than any years that came before or after them. For years I have written poetry in a journal, jotting down little rhymes that capture some slice of life or emotion I am experiencing. Certainly, Emily Dickinson's legacy is safe from any threat by my poetic contributions, but hey, my poems are therapeutic—to me, anyway!

Here's a snippet about my life with Jamie; I'll talk more about it later:

Every time I look at you
I see
Bittersweet memories of you and me
Precious moments that we shared from the start

What returns for me in the memory of those five years is the "sweet," an oasis of calm and happiness in our often-turbulent life together. The "bitter" would revisit our lives in time. I've always found comfort in the saying, "This, too, shall pass," especially in difficult times, because it suggests that at some point, the pages turn on our darkest days. The problem is, sometimes you don't want anything to change, and it does anyway.

Me and my beautiful children, early days.

seven

WITNESSING A MIRACLE

One moment your life is neat and predictable, with everything in its place, and then a windstorm blows through, and you are left wondering what hit you. Things are never the same again.

On a cool, crisp October morning, I had no idea that a huge storm would rage through my life that day. It started out just like any other morning. I sipped my coffee at 5:30 a.m., reading my devotional as I always do. Jamie joined me briefly before shooting out the door to work by 6 a.m. Bryan, who was nine at the time, and Britney, then four, woke to a hot breakfast at 6:30; forty-five minutes later, Bryan was on the school bus on his way to third grade, and Britney and I were on our way to the day care I owned and operated.

The children at my day care followed an unsurprising pattern: activities and snack in the morning, and then lunch at noon, followed by story time, when the little ones would lie on their mats and listen to one of the teachers or me read a story until they fell asleep. I was just finishing a story that day when Sandra, who worked with me at the day care as a secretary, poked her head in the preschool room and indicated that I should come talk to her immediately.

34

"I just got a call from Bryan's school," she said. "They said to pick him up immediately, because he's very ill."

Cold dread filled my entire body. I raced to the school and ran inside to the office, where I found my son lying on his side on the floor. I knelt beside him, and when I put my hands on him, I could feel that his body was as stiff as a board. His eyes were open, but they were in a cool, remote stare, as if nothing was registering. Bryan was drooling out the side of his mouth, and he was completely unresponsive to me.

> TERROR NOW COMPETED WITH DREAD AS I DETERMINED WITHIN SECONDS THAT MY SON WAS IN DEEP TROUBLE. "LET'S GO *NOW!*"

Terror now competed with dread. I don't know why the school didn't call an ambulance, but I determined within seconds that my son was in deep trouble. "Let's go *now!*" I yelled at the school secretary, who jumped out of her chair. I picked up my big boy, his body completely rigid, and carried him like a heavy slab of wood to my car, where I laid him in the backseat. For the second time that day, I don't remember being behind the wheel, but I must have been on autopilot.

A Thousand Deaths

When we arrived at the ER, thankfully Bryan's was the only emergency the staff had to attend to. There was a nurse with blonde hair who did triage on Bryan. I pelted her questions.

"What's wrong with him?"

"Why is he so stiff?"

"Is he going to be all right?"

She actually broke out in red welts on her face and neck, partly because I was so persistent, but mostly I think because she hadn't a clue what to say to me, and she knew she couldn't give me the answer I so desperately wanted to hear: *"Yes, don't worry. He'll be just fine."*

After what seemed like hours but was really about twenty minutes, Dr. Shelby Smith arrived, guns blazing, to fire off a bunch of orders to the medical staff. "Give him 20 cc's of this, and 30 cc's of that," he barked. Don't ask me what he was ordering those nurses to give Bryan, but I believe to this day he saved my son's life.

Jamie showed up, frantic, just seconds after Dr. Smith, and together we huddled in the waiting room as Bryan was examined. When Dr. Smith came out a few minutes later, his face was serious. "Bryan had an internal seizure, but now it has passed," he said, adding that now our boy was in a coma.

My brain registered these details to some degree, but I was in a state of shock. How could this be happening? I had sent a healthy boy off to school in the morning, and now he was comatose, his prognosis unclear, and he was about to be airlifted to New Orleans, where he may or may not ever wake up.

A helicopter arrived to take my son to Oschner Hospital. As they transferred Bryan from the ground to the helicopter, with the propeller blades whirring away and medical personnel hustling all around us, I died a thousand deaths. Jamie and I were not permitted to get on that helicopter; only the medics could be onboard with Bryan. Can you imagine what that felt like, to see my unconscious son lifted in the air without me?

Numb, I forced myself to turn away from the sight of the helicopter and concentrate on walking to the car. When Jamie and I walked outside the hospital, there was a crowd of about fifty friends and fellow church members gathered to greet us. Brother Steve Echols from the First Baptist Church had been notified of Bryan's sudden illness, and he immediately organized a large prayer chain.

Because of my day care, just about everyone in town knew our family. I had fifteen employees, and if you weren't working for me, chances were good that we had helped care for your child—I had nearly everyone's kids in town.

Even in my state of shock, I could feel the love and prayers of our community, and those prayers carried us as we drove the hour and a half to the hospital. This was before the days of cell phones, and there was no way to get any information on Bryan's condition. Maybe this was a good thing, because there was no news to be had. At any rate, Jamie and I drove in near silence, each mile clicking off on the odometer bringing us that much closer to our son—and news of his fate.

When we got to Oschner Hospital, Bryan was still unconscious, and he would remain that way until eleven o'clock the next morning, when we were notified that he had woken up. When I walked into his room, Bryan was sitting up in bed, eating a red Popsicle.

"Where am I, Mama?" he said. I burst into tears and hugged him as tightly as I dared, relief flooding over me.

Within a day, Bryan was released from the hospital, and we brought our son home, never to take his life—or the life of anyone we loved—for granted again. As Bryan grew up, there were many reminders of this.

Hitting the Highlights

My son was a fire starter, a daredevil, and at some point during his childhood it seemed as if he broke every bone in his body. I am just hitting the highlights here!

The year before his seizure, when he was eight, Bryan had been in a dirt bike accident. I had heard the crash, and when I ran to his crumpled body, the first thing I saw was that his limbs were not lying in a natural position. The second thing I could see was that blood was pouring out of his ears. *Brain injury.* It was all I could think of, and my heart froze in my chest.

"Don't cry, Mama," Bryan said, blood running all over his face and everywhere. "I'll be all right."

He broke his leg, his arm, and all kinds of bones in his hand, but thank the Lord, there was no brain injury.

For months afterward, he was in a half body cast at home, and between me and the pastor's wife, we helped him keep up with his schoolwork at home.

That was not the last trauma to be had as a result of that motorbike. A year after Bryan's seizure, when he was about ten, he fell while riding, and the bike's exhaust pipe landed on his leg, badly burning him. For months afterward, he had to go in for treatments, and they would scrub his burn to clean it so it would heal properly. It was excruciating, and poor Bryan would scream his head off while I sat there holding his hand, taking deep breaths and praying so I wouldn't start screaming too.

I never knew what was going to happen to Bryan on any given day. All I knew was that the two of us were too well acquainted with the medical personnel in our area. He also had asthma, which meant many doctor's visits over the course of his childhood. In fact, when Bryan had his seizure and word spread, five doctors left their own practices and came to the ER that day to see if they could help. They all knew us so well.

When we checked out of Oschner Hospital, no one really had any tight theories about why Bryan had had such a life-endangering seizure. I have always thought his asthma medications were responsible in some way. We had to have his blood levels checked regularly, to make sure nothing was out of balance, and I think he was playing hard on the playground that day and got overheated, triggering his seizure.

Dr. Smith was amazed there had been no permanent brain damage, as Bryan had been without oxygen for a dangerous amount of time. He had no medical explanation for it whatsoever. No one knew what was wrong with Bryan, and at first, no one knew how to treat him. But God knew, and that day he listened to the prayers of his people—our friends, family, community, and church members, and I'm guessing even total strangers—and answered by preserving my son.

Bryan is thirty-one years old today, healthy and strong. They told us years ago that someone who has a seizure of the type Bryan had is prone to have another one. But he never did.

I will always believe that on that day, twenty-two years ago now, we encountered more than a windstorm; we witnessed a miracle.

Britney, Bryan, and I at a charity auction at Planet Hollywood.

eight

FRIENDSHIPS

In the 2000 census, the population of Kentwood, Louisiana, was 2,205 people, broken down into 805 households and 559 families. We are one of them.

You can say what you want about small towns being boring or backward, but there is no place on earth I would rather be than Kentwood. To this day, that town is a haven, a cradle for our family no matter what has gone on in our sometimes crazy lives. When our days are bleak and dark, we come home to find people who knew us and loved us before our lives got caught up in the twister of fame and reckless tabloids and heartless paparazzi.

Here there are no places to nosh on baby lobster tempura, get a hot stone massage, or find the perfect pair of shoes to go with your red carpet dress (the only reddish carpets in town are in the Kentwood Historical Museum, in front of a scale model of the U.S.S. *Louisiana*!). Even still, Kentwood beats the pants off of LA. Here I find Miss Nyla's to-die-for corn bread and greens, Uncle James's big bear hug, and the perfect pair of rubber boots from the feed store to wear while working in my garden. Here I can count on the fact that Miss Hazel, my mother's best friend and a fellow war bride from England, will always bake and decorate the perfect birthday cakes for my children on their birthdays, and that she will still charge me twelve dollars per cake, same as always. Here I find warm smiles, friendly handshakes, and the comforting look in people's eyes that says, *I've known you since you were an itty-bitty girl, and it's always going to be that way.*

I've lived in small towns and big ones, and I've noticed some things about the difference between the two ways of life. It seems to me that individuality is lost when you are just one of the masses, and worse, spirituality can get lost too. In a small town, people know all your business—as if the whole world doesn't know my business anyway!—but then there are always going to be good folks who pray for you by name and who care for you in a personal way.

> IN A SMALL TOWN, PEOPLE KNOW ALL YOUR BUSINESS—AS IF THE WHOLE WORLD DOESN'T KNOW MY BUSINESS ANYWAY!

That care was exemplified to me and my family when those five doctors left their own practices and raced to the ER that terrible day of Bryan's seizure. Later, when my sister, Sandra, was dying, her doctors would come to the house, just to see how she was doing. They were never paid one extra dime but made those house calls out of the goodness of their hearts.

In this old-fashioned soil, my mainstay friendships grew.

Jill, Margaret, Joy, and Kelly

Even when one of our lives takes an unexpected turn and we are separated by time and geography from one another, my four dearest friends and I have never lost the ties that bind us together. I could not have made it through losing my parents and sister, raising my children, bankruptcy, my

Jill and I have been friends ever since Bryan was born. (You do the math!)

husband's alcoholism and rehab, our divorce, and the fallout of my daughters' fame without my dear friends Jill, Margaret, Joy, and Kelly.

At times in my life, I couldn't afford groceries—much less counseling—but those women have been my counselors, and I hope I have been theirs. We have been therapists for one another, sometimes talking things through hours at a time. Thank goodness we are there for each other, "on call" day or night, with a listening ear or some sweet tea and sympathy.

Jill Prescott, my friend I've known the longest, has bailed me out on too many occasions to count. When times were hard financially, Jill would loan me cash. I would insist on writing her a postdated check as goodwill. We did this for six months or more at one point in my life.

If you've seen the movie *Steel Magnolias*, you know who I mean when I mention the Ouiser Boudreaux character, played by Shirley MacLaine in the film. Margaret is my Ouiser, with an unreadable air about her, but a heart of gold. Margaret and I met at the day care I owned and operated, first when she brought her daughter and later when she worked as my secretary.

If Margaret doesn't feel like smiling in a social setting, she just won't smile, even though the rest of us are smiling away just to be polite. There's nothing artificial about Margaret, so she can come across as distant and maybe a touch aloof. But let me tell you, my friend Margaret would move heaven and earth for you—she could never say no to anyone in need. Margaret has offered to shuttle Jamie Lynn to school and ball games when I couldn't; she's even dropped things at her own home to come to mine and run it as I would for a while until I am back in town or whatever the need may be. The best thing about Margaret is that she understands that talking about a problem doesn't always solve it. She has created some healthy distractions for me over the years, so I can say, like that epitome of a Steel Magnolia, Scarlett O' Hara, in times of trouble, "I'll just think about it tomorrow!"

My friends, Kelly, Joy, and Margaret, at a party to launch Britney's tour.

I met Joy fifteen years ago when I started teaching. She was teaching right across the hall. We have been through so much together. She is the friend who will take a bad situation and turn it around. I have so many memories of us laughing and crying at the same time. If you met her, you'd pick up on the "warm and fuzzy" part of her right away. She's very warm and also really funny. We have a knack for getting into funny predicaments together. We refer to ourselves as "Dumb and Dumber," and often silliness prevails when we are together; such is our comfort level in each other's presence. I love Joy because she makes me laugh when I dearly need to do just that.

Last but not least, there's Kelly. You would look at her and think she was beautiful and serious, but she, like Margaret, is not what she seems to the casual observer. When you really get to know her, Kelly is young-hearted and fun. We have taken some of the most mundane experiences of our shared motherhood (our girls Jamie Lynn and Crystal are the same age), and made them some of our most hilarious memories.

Joy, Kelly, and I—the "three musketeer" moms—cheering Leigha, Crystal, and Jamie Lynn at a basketball game.

Jamie Lynn and Crystal played ball together; therefore Kelly and I had to take our turns to work the concessions stand at the games. We would always try to work our designated duties together. If you've ever assembled a hundred hot dogs after a game, you know things can get pretty hectic behind that concessions counter. Kelly and I would slap those orders together as fast as we could, but keep in mind this was not either of our fortes. *Did the guy in the green jacket order a hot dog or a burger? Did that lady say "diet" or did I imagine it?* We often held our breath when the person left, wondering if he would discover in short order that what he asked for was not at all what he received from the inept concession stand staff.

Big crowds of hungry basketball fans made us nervous, and Kelly and I often made a mess filling their orders. One

The gang, including Dinah and Sandy Simms, gathered in Vegas to celebrate the launch of Britney's tour.

time I got impatient with the ketchup bottle, as I kept banging on the bottom of it and nothing was coming out. All of the sudden, half the bottle spewed out in this huge blob, and I looked like a bloody accident victim the rest of the night!

This was just one of our many shared ordeals when Kelly would use her dry humor to get us through. "To quote the Bible," she said, "'It is only for a season.' I hope it's a short one."

My Watchdogs

Since Britney first became well-known, my girlfriends have also become like watchdogs. If a tabloid or entertainment show says something derogatory about me or my family, they become like mama bears. The first one to detect trouble picks up the phone, and soon all four are venting to one another—and conspiring about how to help. When something really bad happens to my family, or any of our families, one or all of them will quietly file into the home of whoever is going through a hard time. We'll hug and cry together, no words needed.

Jill, Margaret, Joy, and Kelly are God's gifts to me. I don't see them every day, and we don't even talk on the phone every day, but whenever we do connect again, somehow we always pick up our friendship right where we left off, close-knit, caring, and essential. Over the years they have become part of me as much as part of my memories. I have always drawn so much strength from them to deal with my family relationships, particularly when

> SINCE BRITNEY FIRST BECAME WELL-KNOWN, MY GIRLFRIENDS HAVE ALSO BECOME LIKE WATCHDOGS. IF A TABLOID OR ENTERTAINMENT SHOW SAYS SOMETHING DEROGATORY ABOUT ME OR MY FAMILY, THEY BECOME LIKE MAMA BEARS.

what should have been the closest relationship in my life—my marriage—was falling apart.

Sherrie

Other close friends have enriched my life over the years, women who have come into my life through various paths and whose friendship exists in another orbit from the one I share with Jill, Margaret, Joy, and Kelly. Sherrie, for example, is my friend who takes such good care of my house for me when I'm gone. She helps me keep the big old place clean, and I don't know how I would cope without her. Sherrie is the kind of person who is wonderful in a crisis; she just steps in and rolls up her sleeves and starts helping. Years ago, I left a candle burning one night, and the living room caught on fire. My dogs barked and barked, waking me even before the smoke alarm, but not before I had inhaled enough smoke to send me to the ER. Jamie Lynn had a friend over for a sleepover, and thank God they woke up in the nick of time; the two girls suffered no smoke inhalation.

The next day, Sherrie came over and cleaned the house as well as she could after the firemen had left—a huge job, and one I was unable to cope with after coming home from the hospital. She drew me a bath and insisted I sleep as long as I needed to, while she stayed with the girls until they woke up.

Jackie

I met Jackie on the first day on set of Jamie Lynn's show *Zoey 101*. Paul, her only child, played Jamie Lynn's younger brother. Nickelodeon was filming at Pepperdine University, and we sat outside on the campus grounds, watching them film the first take of the kids arriving at the fictional school. Jackie and I connected from the beginning, though she was a little shy on our first meeting, hesitating a bit before she spoke. I found that sweet and endearing.

Sometimes when people first meet me, they are apprehensive—at least those who happen to know I'm Britney's mom—and no doubt they have a bundle of preconceived ideas about who I am. I come across—or should I say I *try* to come across?—as a very self-confident person. But if people spend a little more time with me, they find out I'm quite the contrary. Jackie seemed to grasp very early on that there was a flesh-and-blood woman behind the mythological monster the tabloids had created, and I sensed I could trust this gentle, kind woman.

Jackie and her husband owned a boutique at the time called Baby Unique, and, as this was during the time Britney was expecting Preston, Jackie helped Britney decorate his nursery. As days on the set got longer, and the children stayed busy, Jackie

> JACKIE SEEMED TO GRASP VERY EARLY ON THAT THERE WAS A FLESH-AND-BLOOD WOMAN BEHIND THE MYTHOLOGICAL MONSTER THE TABLOIDS HAD CREATED.

and I became closer and closer. She became my one and only confidante in LA, and we shared everything with each other. I used to tease Jackie and say she was my walking navigation system. I could be lost anywhere in the city, call her, and be on my way in the right direction.

I had no idea back on the first day of filming *Zoey 101* that God would use Jackie in a mighty way in my life. God is very strategic. Only he knew how much I would need and depend on the strength and companionship of this dear friend years later, when it was time to fight for my older daughter's life and outsmart the foes put in place by Satan himself.

nine

THE OTHER WOMAN

If you don't face something when it is happening, you will have to face it later on. That is a lesson that took me years to learn.

One of the hardest things I ever had to face was the fact that Jamie was drinking too much again, even after being a wonderful husband and father for five years. People ask me if there was some sort of trigger, a traumatic event that pushed Jamie back into drinking. The answer is no. Really, when I look back, what I see is a slow, almost insidious slide from his having a beer at a cookout to being a man in the dark grip of addiction, reckless, sometimes mean, and absent from his family, physically and emotionally.

It started out innocently enough, with Jamie enjoying a casual drink at our crawfish boils or parties. Obviously, he could handle a drink or two here and there, or so we thought. It was just that kind of social drinking that ended up pulling Jamie and all of us beneath that undertow of alcoholism again. We thought he could get away with it, but in reality, an addict like Jamie couldn't handle even one drink very well.

He started drinking more and more, and I started to try to manage his intake. This is also textbook conduct on the part of the alcoholic's spouse. We talked a lot about not letting his drinking get out of control again, about how it would be okay if he only drank wine, or if he only drank beer and not anything harder. Then it became, "If you only drink after work," and "If you only drink with me and not your buddies," and so on and so on. Pretty soon our efforts to maintain Jamie's drinking at a reasonable level were almost ridiculous. We worked harder at controlling his alcohol consumption than we did maintaining our marriage.

> PRETTY SOON OUR EFFORTS TO MAINTAIN JAMIE'S DRINKING AT A REASONABLE LEVEL WERE ALMOST RIDICULOUS. WE WORKED HARDER AT CONTROLLING HIS ALCOHOL CONSUMPTION THAN WE DID MAINTAINING OUR MARRIAGE.

This is classic codependent behavior. I reacted to Jamie's disease with a diseased pattern of conduct myself. By making excuses for him, feeling sorry for him, and shielding him from the negative consequences of his drinking, I was in some ways enabling his condition. I thought I was getting by, coping as best I could under the circumstances—that we all were—but really we were barely hanging on, sick ourselves from the unhealthy construct of our family life. It's been said that alcoholism is a family disease, and I was ailing in my own way as I got caught up in his drinking—specifically where, when, and how much he was doing it.

Sometimes only a crisis (or a bunch of them) can break through denial.

Jamie started neglecting his business. He was overspending, and things started falling apart. He would travel to work out of town, and I was left to face the bill collectors. It was a game, a toss, to figure out how to keep the wolf away from the door. I would make one phone call to try to keep the lights on, followed by another call to the phone company to try to persuade them not to turn the phone off—again. I was robbing Peter to pay Paul, as they say. Literally, sometimes I didn't know how we would put gas in the car or food on the table. I was always making excuses for Jamie, covering for him with the bill collectors, with his work, telling them he couldn't come in because he was sick or something had suddenly come up.

I lived every day in uncertainty and insecurity. I woke up every morning thinking, *Did Jamie come home last night?* Or if he had been around somewhat dependably for a while, I'd wonder, *Is this the day the man I love will start drinking again?* Or, *What will he be like when he comes home this weekend?* Or, *How long will this binge last?* Or, *Will there be enough money to buy essentials?* Or, *Which creditors will I have to fend off today?* Or, *Who will I have to make excuses to on Jamie's behalf?* Or, *How long will it be before he acts like a daddy again?* Or sometimes some version of all of the above, almost all at once.

The sad truth is, you can't make excuses to the most important people of all: your children. You just cannot cover with your kids. In an alcoholic family, you can't hide the truth of things from them, because often they are more attuned to the problem than you are. Sometimes I was in denial about something Jamie had told me, something I dearly wanted to believe about where he was and what he was really doing. More than a few times, my children would call me on it.

"Mama, you can't be that blind," they would say, and I would feel so naive for believing Jamie. Of course, I wanted to believe him from the pit of my soul.

After one particularly nasty binge that led to a blowout between us, I slumped down on the kitchen floor and cried my eyes out.

"You know I love you, don't you?" Jamie said to me, his voice ragged with emotion and regret.

"I know you love me," I said wearily. "That's never been the point. But it's the way that you love me—it's a destructive love. I'd rather not be in love at all than be in love this way."

Sometimes I wondered who on earth I was becoming. Who was this controlling, angry woman who looked back at me in the mirror? One day I lost it, hauling out an ice chest from the back of Jamie's pickup truck and shooting it to smithereens.

It was Jamie's Grandma Lexie's birthday, and we were getting ready to go as a family to a pizza buffet in McComb to celebrate with her. I had asked Jamie many times that day if he had been drinking, and in my codependent way, I just kept asking even though the answer was obvious. The final straw was when Jamie stumbled out of the bedroom and staggered in front of a mirror to check his appearance. *Busted*. I was livid. I went out in the backyard and told Jamie's brother, Austin, to haul out the ice chest in Jamie's pickup truck and put it in the backyard. The chest was full of booze. I had a shotgun—we Southern girls know our way around a weapon—and I started firing before Austin was as far out of the way as he would have liked. "Whoa! Hey!" Jamie's big, muscular brother did a little "get out of Dodge" dance. And then I blasted that chest to smithereens.

I shot his beer.

I shot his wine.

And I think in a very real way I shot the "other woman," the mistress who had stolen my husband from me.

You know what they say about desperate times.

Our health spa and gym was right next door, and a lady was on her way in to work out when she heard me firing. She thought I was shooting a snake or something, and came over and asked if everything was okay.

"Nothing's okay," I said calmly. "I am just killing the beer in this chest." Minutes later, I collected my family—including my drunken husband—and drove off to the pizza buffet. It was life as usual in the Spears family.

Even then, I stuck by Jamie. People say that I could have or should have left him a long time before I did, but they have no idea what it was like. Anyone who is married to an alcoholic knows that a drinker can convince you time and time again that he can overcome his problem . . . *this time.* Our family life was like a huge roller-coaster ride in some ways, but when we were at the top of the ride, life was great. When Jamie was good, he was *really* good, attentive, sweet, fun, wonderful . . . and he convinced me countless times that he was going to stay that way.

I let him get away with so much because he could. When I look back, I wish I'd had the strength to say, "That's it. We're done until you can prove to me that your behavior has really and truly changed." I wish I could have trusted that I could stand on my own two feet with God helping me.

But it's a terrifying feeling to throw away everything when you've tried so hard to make it work. I was also worried about finances. I didn't know if I could make it on my own, even though I had my day-care business, and later, my teaching job. I thought, *Where am I going to live?* And, *How will it work with the kids?* I was afraid to move, so I stayed put, stymied by indecision. Also, divorce seemed to me to be the greater of two evils at the time. It didn't strike me as the answer.

Our bank account was empty, and so were my emotional stores. I had Bryan and Britney to take care of, and I was completely reliant on God's care. At my darkest, emptiest hours, I knew God held me in his strong hands. He had me, and it would be okay.

> AT MY DARKEST, EMPTIEST HOURS, I KNEW GOD HELD ME IN HIS STRONG HANDS. HE HAD ME, AND IT WOULD BE OKAY.

People say I was strong, but that wasn't it, not at all. Trust me, I had moments of precarious, terrifying weakness that could have gone one way or the other, many times. But I felt at the core of my being that if I, as a mother to those precious children, fell apart, they would fall apart too. A mother has to do whatever it takes to keep things from crashing and burning for her family.

Looking back, I'm almost positive staying with Jamie was not the right thing to do for the kids. Our children saw far too many knock-down, drag-out fights between their mama and daddy. But I kept going, fueled by a mother's dogged, foundational desire—mistaken though it was—to do the best by her children. Most of all, I wanted them to know that somehow it would all be okay, that God held us all. I wanted to project an attitude of hope and good things to come. They would be okay too, I prayed, if only they believed that.

ten

BRITNEY STARTS SINGING

As a child, Britney was almost another appendage for me.

I could never be without her, even if I wanted to; she was such a mama's girl, from the very start. When she was little and involved in gymnastics, Britney had to be able to see me through the window of the gym where she and the other kids would be doing cartwheels and splits and somersaults, or she would burst into tears. I had to be careful, because Britney could pick up on my thoughts and moods without me saying a word. In the years to come, when she would be in some far-flung place across the world from me, she and I would at times have this sixth sense that something was going on with the other; if it was me, my phone would ring and it would be Britney, wondering what was wrong.

I don't know why my little girl and I were so connected. We just were.

When all my children were three years old, I wrote them a poem expressing my hopes and dreams for them. Here is a piece of the poem I wrote for Britney:

BRITNEY STARTS SINGING

Sometimes when I see
The sparkle in her eye
It makes me sad
I want to cry
Cruel world turn away
Spare my little star
Let her wit and charming beauty
Go very far

When I look back at those words, I honestly have no idea how I "knew" certain things were going to happen. I am no prophet, yet people have pointed out that my poem seems to see into the future. All I knew was that I had a charming and talented little girl whom I loved more than life itself. As her mom, Britney was a "star" to me. The line "Cruel world turn away / Spare my little star" especially hits a nerve today. After years of seeing how fame brings with it unrelenting pressure, the always-present paparazzi, and endless criticism from the media, I know just how cruel the world can be.

But when Britney was a young girl, all of the negative aspects of fame were light-years away. In fact, fame was nothing I ever imagined would happen to any of us. I was just living my life, enjoying the every-day events at our house that now seem so precious, like all the times Britney and Laura Lynne would play mommies in the little playhouse we had built for them. Britney preferred baby dolls over Barbie dolls any day of the week—she was a nurturing soul from the start.

And she absolutely loved to dance. By the time she was two, she was dancing all over the house, so I decided to sign her up for lessons to give her an outlet for her constant movement. At three, she was the leader of the pack. At her first dance recital, her job was to lead all the other little dancers onstage in the right position. All the little girls would lean over during the dance to look at Britney to make sure they were doing the right steps. She was always so sure of herself.

When she was four years old, her dance teacher wanted her to do a solo dance at the recital. It was the first time Britney was singled out in that way. I just stepped back and watched, proud, of course, but also somewhat puzzled as to where she got those natural gifts as a dancer. They certainly weren't from me!

Britney could sing too. From the time she was a toddler, she would sing along with me or the car radio or theme songs piping out of the television set. Even then, I thought she had a strong voice for such a little girl, but then again, mothers are biased creatures, aren't they? As it turned out, though, people other than me started to notice Britney's singing voice and her obvious joy in performing around anyone who would listen.

> PEOPLE OTHER THAN ME STARTED TO NOTICE BRITNEY'S SINGING VOICE AND HER OBVIOUS JOY IN PERFORMING AROUND ANYONE WHO WOULD LISTEN.

If I had a nickel for every time I heard someone tell me Britney was "Broadway bound," I'd be wrapped in a towel someplace hot, waiting for my spa treatment right now.

There was another "if I had a nickel" statement too: many people who heard Britney sing or saw her dance would look me in the eye and say, "Your daughter has a gift." Some of them even said—out loud—part two of that sentence: "What are *you* going to do about it?" What was I going to do to help my gifted child achieve her potential?

I didn't really think it through, to be honest. I shuttled her to lessons and the occasional competition, I flipped through a thousand magazines, and I drank a thousand cups of bad coffee as I waited for her to get done—just like any other soccer mom or gymnastics mom. I would have rather been back home, cooking dinner, cleaning my house, and spending time with my family, but that's how I supported Britney in what she wanted to do. As with Bryan's sports, if Britney's gymnastics and dancing didn't interfere too much with our family life, I would try to accommodate those things. And Britney was absolutely determined to do it all. If she had been in charge, no doubt we would have been out every night and every weekend at dance recitals and gymnastics competitions. She was extremely driven for a young girl, tenacious in her desire to be the best at what she loved.

The same time she was starting to compete in dancing and singing, Britney was really getting into gymnastics. She was trying to keep up both her dancing and her gymnastics, and, I'll tell you, it wasn't working—not one little bit. Any parent who has tried to juggle too many interests at once for a child knows what I mean. We had to have a talk.

"Baby," I said when I sat her down one day, "you can't do both gymnastics and dancing and singing. It's killing you and it's killing me. You have to choose one."

She chose dancing and singing.

Unstoppable

One year, when she was just five or six, Britney won a singing and dancing competition at Dairy Days, a local festival we have here in our dairy-intensive area of Louisiana. I had to be right there on the side of the stage so she knew I was there.

Dance teachers and others started to take more notice of Britney, suggesting that she compete at other talent competitions. All of the competitions were within an hour's drive, so it didn't seem like that big of a deal.

One time I took her to Lafayette, Louisiana, to a talent competition. There were so many contestants. I was warned to keep Britney away from a certain little girl. The girl's mother had taught her daughter to intimidate whoever was her biggest competitor. The girl had pinched

Britney the last time she was in a competition with her! This time, though, she marched up to my daughter and told her, "You're not any good. I'm going to win today no matter what you do." Britney didn't say a word. Instead, she strode right up on that stage and sang as if she was Aretha Franklin, though the song itself was probably "Sweet Georgia Brown" or "Harvest Moon." My itty-bitty girl belted out that song with a voice that filled every crevice of that theater with the biggest, most clear-pitched sound ever. She won, hands down, but I was much more proud of how she handled herself in that intimidating situation. I cried to see that little forceful angel get out on that stage and take control.

When Britney was about eight, we got talked into doing a "Little Miss Something" beauty pageant, because there was supposedly an emphasis on talent over looks in this one. *Right.* I should have known better. I had never wanted her near one of those things, because the way they were set up seemed so unfair to some children. While a young girl could work hard to make her leap higher or her steps more precise, there was nothing much she could do to improve the countenance God gave her.

> WHEN BRITNEY WAS ABOUT EIGHT, WE GOT TALKED INTO DOING A "LITTLE MISS SOMETHING" BEAUTY PAGEANT, BECAUSE THERE WAS SUPPOSEDLY AN EMPHASIS ON TALENT OVER LOOKS IN THIS ONE. *RIGHT.* I SHOULD HAVE KNOWN BETTER.

The pageant lived up to my fears. The mothers were awful backstage, primping their daughters and bickering among themselves. I was horrified by the whole thing. Of course, since we were completely green about the pageant system, I put her in the wrong dress (it didn't even fit properly) and the wrong kind of socks. Britney ended up placing near the bottom, and the poor little thing was in tears. A friend of mine said we should try one more. "You can't let this child end on this note," she told me. "She'll never feel pretty again, and her mama always told her she was the most beautiful girl in the world."

I wanted Britney to feel good about herself because of who she was and how she treated people, not because some silly pageant told her she was or was not pretty enough. I emphasized the team dance competition troupe she was in with other girls, which brought out her best qualities of friendship and leadership and hard work. As a mom, I felt good about those competitions because she could work hard and get better, with her teammates and her helping one another to be their best.

The interesting thing about Britney is that she was always—and I do mean *always*—highly motivated to excel. She raised the bar for herself and went after whatever goal or level of excellence she set her mind to. Never once did I have to get on her case to practice. Never. If anything, she practiced so much it drove me crazy. I would say, "Baby, just relax for a minute or two, please—you're making *me* tired!" But day after day, week after week, year after year during that era, Britney would be wearing out the floor with her dance steps and tearing off the roof of our house, singing the latest hit by Whitney Houston, Mariah Carey, or Madonna. She was, in a word, unstoppable.

Stage Mom?

People always want to know how I "got" Britney on the path to stardom, as if I held some kind of magical secret for leading a child down that glittering corridor to fame and fortune. Trust me, I have no such secrets! To be totally honest, we just stumbled on the dancing path, and one thing kind of led to another. Little-girl dance lessons led to small (very small) local competitions, which then resulted in slightly bigger regional competitions. The farther afield we would travel, the more new faces we would meet, and some of those new people would hear Britney sing, and they would suggest another competition. And so it went, very gradually growing in terms of the level of talent and the stakes that went along with it. As long as it didn't interfere with our family life or our work schedules, I was willing to do my part to support my daughter's dreams. And Britney dreamed big dreams.

This is probably the part where I should defend myself from the claims that I was a pushy stage mother, prodding my unwilling child from one audition to the next.

To be honest, I am always a little startled when I hear that's what folks think about me. I'm somewhat oblivious sometimes. Trust me, in this crazy world of Hollywood and tabloids, "oblivious" is an excellent quality to cultivate! And quite frankly, it's a waste of ink to defend myself, because people will believe what they want to believe anyway. The worst connotation of the archetypical stage mom is that she dreams up fame and fortune at any cost for her child, knowing all along that her ambition is for herself. I've seen moms like this since Britney was a little girl (the pincher's mother is a prime example), and they always make me cringe for their children. I wanted to help along my child and her dreams, but I was also reluctant to jump in the deep end when I didn't really know who or what would be swimming in the pool alongside us.

I had no idea someday we would be awash in sharks.

eleven

HERE COMES JAMIE LYNN

My friend Margaret walked in my door, unannounced, on a dark day years ago. I didn't know what she was doing there, but even in the gloomy state I was in, I could see she was on a mission. I burst into tears to see that woman roll in with all her gusto.

"C'mon," she said gently, motioning me up from my rocking chair, where I was rocking my newborn daughter, Jamie Lynn. Margaret didn't ask any questions; she just picked up the baby from my arms, grabbed the diaper bag, and strode out the door. I had no choice but to follow.

Very few words passed between my friend and me as we drove out of my driveway and down the road. We stopped at Sonic to get soft drinks and then drove to Margaret's house for a sandwich. When she returned the two of us to our house, and I sat back down in that rocking chair, I realized something: my problems were still there, but somehow they didn't hurt as much.

Nine months earlier, we got the shock of our lives when I found out I was expecting our third child. Bryan was a teenager, and Britney was almost ten years old. Jamie and I thought we were done with having kids, and there's no way we would have planned to bring another child into our messy lives at that point. Jamie's vasectomy underscored this notion considerably. Turns out he never went back to the doctor for that all-important follow-up appointment!

I was running the day care, which was a blessing but still required much of my energy and time. Jamie's business, though, was faltering to the point that, despite the stability of the day care, our finances were in dire straits. The day care did not make enough money to pay all the household bills plus cover for shortfalls in Jamie's business. My mama was very ill with arthritis, and though that time period was relatively stable in terms of Jamie's drinking, alcoholism still hung over our family like a heavy, dark backdrop.

God knew how much we all needed Jamie Lynn in our lives. Years later, when Britney was surprised by her pregnancy with Jayden, I could speak from experience when I told her that these "unplanned" babies are the ones the Lord himself insists on being here. They are his plan, not ours. Like Jayden, Jamie Lynn has been dearly loved and has been a great bonus gift to her family.

As my pregnancy progressed, and I became more comfortable with the idea of being a mother again—and even a little bit excited—my worries also grew. How would we even pay for this baby's birth in the hospital when we didn't have health insurance?

Bryan and Britney were thrilled. Of course, a ten-year-old, baby doll-loving girl would be excited to have a new sibling, but even fourteen-year-old Bryan was over the moon for his baby sister. Then again, he was the kind of boy who would kiss me on the cheek when I would walk into a basketball game, while his friends sitting in the bleachers didn't even acknowledge their mothers. He was always goo-goo over Jamie Lynn. We all were, and still are.

On April 4, 1991, Jamie Lynn Spears was born via C-section. Her first name honors her daddy, and her second name is after me. And as new life always does, the beautiful baby in our arms represented a fresh start.

But we still had our problems, and money was at the top of the list. Thank goodness it hadn't occurred to me that I would have to have a C-section, because of course C-sections are far more expensive than a natural delivery. Little by little, we were able to pay the hospital back, but it took a long time.

Overdoing It

About eight days after Jamie Lynn was born, I had been feeling tired, naturally, and was still sore around my incision site, although I didn't think there was anything wrong with me beyond the normal sleepless nights every mother of a newborn experiences. One day, I was wandering around the house, holding my baby in one arm and rummaging around with my other, searching for a missing piece of one of Britney's dance costumes. Suddenly, I felt a gush of warmth, and I looked down to see that I was standing in a pool of blood. I called for Jamie to come, and I slumped down to the floor. Clearly, I was hemorrhaging.

Jamie picked me up and carried me to the car. There was blood everywhere, and Britney was crying, scared to death about what was happening to me. While I was hospitalized overnight, the doctors told me I had been overdoing it after my C-section, and that had caused me to hemorrhage. I tried to take it easier on myself after that, having learned the hard way what can happen when you don't.

Family of Five

Bryan and Britney were a huge help with Jamie Lynn, especially Britney. At ten, she and Laura Lynne were devoted little "mommies" to the baby, helping me rock her, dress her, and feed her. When I was close by, I would allow them to take Jamie Lynn into their playhouse, which was set up like a miniature house with a kitchen and an ironing board and little beds. Britney and Laura Lynne had a real, live baby to play house with, and they loved every minute of it.

Bryan, Parkland Academy's quarterback, giving a pep talk at the pep rally before a game.

Bryan was very active in sports, and we spent hours going to his basketball, baseball, and football games. If we weren't sitting on the bleachers somewhere, we were invariably at one of Britney's dance lessons and recitals. Being a mother to Bryan, Britney, and Jamie Lynn, I was in my element, maybe more than at any other time before or since. When I see younger women these days who are raising young children, carpooling and packing lunches and going on field trips, I am jealous! I loved everything about being a mother. In the midst of Jamie's alcoholism and the constant uncertainty that goes along with a loved one's addiction, motherhood kept me focused, if not sane.

I tried hard to cook healthy meals and keep a clean, orderly house. I sought out the best schools and church programs for my kids, and I happily shuttled them to sports events, dance, karate—you name it—not to mention to their friends' houses for play dates.

> WHEN I SEE YOUNGER WOMEN THESE DAYS WHO ARE RAISING YOUNG CHILDREN, CARPOOLING AND PACKING LUNCHES AND GOING ON FIELD TRIPS, I AM JEALOUS! I LOVED EVERYTHING ABOUT BEING A MOTHER.

Some say mothers lose themselves when they raise children, that they become too absorbed with their little ones to pay any attention to themselves. Maybe some do. All I know is, being a mother is who I am. I loved rocking my babies, baking cookies, reading stories, and snuggling with my children and a tub of popcorn and watching the latest Disney movie. I remember with such fondness things such as first haircuts, when my children learned to swim or ride a bike, and the first and last days of school, because those were the monumental moments of my life too.

You may be thinking, *Gee, Lynne Spears sure didn't have much of a life in those days.* But I'll tell you what, it was the life of my dreams, and I would give anything to live that life all over again.

An Old Soul

I think of Jamie Lynn as my own miracle baby, a child who was really not supposed to be here but she came anyway, the loveliest, most unexpected gift of my life. She has been an old soul since day one, my most reserved, private child.

Now, that's not to say she was a serene baby. Jamie Lynn could never sit still. One time my mama watched Jamie Lynn run circles around us when she was a toddler. "Lynne," she said, "you've got to take care of yourself, because you know no one can run after that one!" My youngest child always knew exactly what she wanted, what she believed, and how she would live out those beliefs. And she had (and has) a will of iron ore. If Jamie Lynn wanted something, she was a force of nature, strong, resilient, and competent.

Jamie Lynn came to this earth with a mission in mind, and the future will tell us the rest of the story.

Adorable three-year-old Jamie Lynn.

twelve

TEACHING

◈

When Jamie Lynn was just two, I made the transition from a job I liked—running the day care—to a career I loved. My desire for that career began many years ago. When it was time for me to go to high school, my parents insisted that I transfer from the local school system and attend a private Catholic girls' boarding school, St. Mary of the Pines, in Magnolia, Missouri, about twenty minutes away from our farm. I didn't want to leave my school friends, and I put up quite a fuss, but it was no use. We weren't even Catholic! But that argument, like all the others, held no water with Daddy and Mama. My parents valued learning, and they felt I would receive a better education there, and that was that—they put their collective foot down.

At first, I felt like a complete outsider at the school. I attended as a day student, among mostly boarding school girls, so that didn't help. St. Mary's was set in a thick forest just up the hill from the Tangipahoa River, and classes were held in dignified, old buildings. The rarefied atmosphere there threw me for a loop, and at first I was a bit of a loner, concentrating on my studies and hanging out with other girls who also didn't fit in with the popular crowd.

But there was one big benefit at St. Mary of the Pines: Sister Patrick, the English teacher I absolutely adored. In her classes, my love for books was deepened, as was my love for learning. I dreamed of becoming an English teacher, like Sister Patrick, someday, or maybe even a college professor. A seed was planted in those English classes, as young ladies in crisp school uniforms discussed Austen and Shakespeare and Hawthorne.

Many years later, the school closed down and became a retreat center for retired nuns. I am proud to be an alumna, for so many reasons, including the fact that St. Mary of the Pines Retreat Center provided refuge for evacuees from Hurricane Katrina, including about fifteen sisters.

Dream Come True

In 1993, the seed sown in Sister Patrick's classes grew into a dream come true: I became a teacher myself. Silver Creek Elementary hired me as their second-grade teacher, a post I would hold for seven years.

A yearbook photo of me and my class; my teaching experience was one of the best times of my life.

I had been running my day care for about ten years at that point, and it was the best business in the world for me to do. We had fifteen employees, and I was friends with all of them. At business school, they may tell you this is not the way to run a tight ship, but what I discovered was that the more of a personal touch I gave to my employees, the more loyal they were to me. I used to have a very relaxed policy when it came to using sick time or personal time. "If you can't come in, you don't even have to call me," I would tell them. "Just find your own replacement." All of my employees had children, and goodness knows, anything can happen with little ones around. I also had young children, so I could relate! They really seemed to appreciate my empathy for their situations, and no one ever abused my policy, not even once.

Even though I thoroughly enjoyed my day care business, in my heart I needed something more to satisfy my mind and fulfill my spirit. I wanted to teach. My preschool and kindergarten at the day care used A Beka, a rigorous, Christian-based curriculum used by top private schools and by many homeschoolers. As a result, those little ones were well prepared to enter first grade as emerging readers, and most of them achieved just that. That was fulfilling to me, of course, but it wasn't exactly what I wanted to do with my teaching background.

Some people were put on this earth to be humanitarians, actors, writers, nurses—whatever it is that feeds their soul and meets that need within to do what they were called to do. Besides motherhood, my primary vocation, teaching met that need for me.

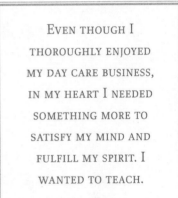

EVEN THOUGH I THOROUGHLY ENJOYED MY DAY CARE BUSINESS, IN MY HEART I NEEDED SOMETHING MORE TO SATISFY MY MIND AND FULFILL MY SPIRIT. I WANTED TO TEACH.

I absolutely loved working with children, first of all, which is key! I loved all types of kids—the smart, sweet children and even the challenging ones who made most teachers want to pull their hair out. Sometimes the principal would purposefully put students in my class who were considered a handful. I took this to be a compliment of my teaching skills, or maybe it was simply a matter of him off-loading a hard case or two to a teacher with less seniority. It didn't matter—I loved them all as they came to me.

If you are not an organized person, you will be forced to become one when you become a teacher. I was always fairly organized, but with up to thirty children to teach and multiple subjects to cover, I had to step it up. A core element of teaching is record keeping, not just of the child's work and grades, but of the various state requirements. All of this regulation helped me improve my orderliness quite a bit. I know I'm a bit of a neat freak, but to this day I love to set things in order.

Another gift of my teaching career was and is undoubtedly Joy, one of my dearest friends and a woman who lives up to her name every day. Joy and I met just before I started teaching, in the hallway outside our classrooms. She was jealous of my room, she told me, because it was bigger and had a sink and a small project area for my students. What a difference the small things make in the classroom! We were instant kindred spirits. Joy has a smile as wide as the Mississippi River, and her sweet voice could melt the hardest heart. Her passionate spirituality and zest for life spill over into mine, and I am so grateful for her friendship.

Joy's daughter, Leigha, and Jamie Lynn are the same age, and they grew up together, becoming as close as their mothers are to each other. Joy and I have known each other for about fifteen years now, but it seems as if we have always known each other. Some people think we are sisters, because we favor each other physically, but more than that, we are alike in our mannerisms, sayings, and gestures. We even finish each other's sentences.

Joy and I love it when someone asks if we are sisters, because then we can have a little fun with that poor person. "Who do you think is older?" we'll ask, watching as the victim scrambles for a diplomatic answer. Most are too polite to call it as they see it, but I am older by a long shot.

I miss those days teaching with Joy right across the hall. We used to love decorating our classrooms with seasonal motifs—leaves, snowflakes, bunnies and chicks—after hours and just gabbing away about every topic under the sun, telling stories from a seemingly endless well.

Teaching was perfect for me. One of the great regrets of my life is quitting in 2000 to go on tour with Britney. Don't get me wrong. It was the right thing to do at the time. But I miss teaching, and I look back on those seven years of teaching as being some of the most satisfying of my life thus far. What could be more gratifying than guiding a seven-year-old student in finally cracking the code of reading? Or providing warmth and nurturing for a child who struggles at home? You simply can't put a price tag on those kinds of rewards.

I remember one little boy so vividly, a very shy and sweet child who was such a strong writer for his age. In this good ol' boy area, it wasn't really a macho thing for a boy to love English, and he seemed to need some extra encouragement to sustain his interest in books and writing. Today, that boy is an English professor, and his mother has told me more than once that I helped him discover his love for English back in the second grade. Do you know how much that means to me?

It's also pleasing to see some of my students all grown up today, attending college or maybe even married themselves and pursuing their own dreams. Scary, because it makes me feel old, but pleasing! But seriously, I am always happy to see my former students, yet a little bit sad too.

Where has the time gone? If I sound wistful, it's because I am. When I quit teaching, my fulfilling, orderly life flew out the window. In its place was a reality I never could have imagined, an existence that would be at times the very antithesis of fulfillment and order.

thirteen

WHY DID I SAY YES?

❧

Why did I say yes to Britney's career? This is the question that has been posed to me by lots of different people over the years. Of course, folks are curious about why I seemingly allowed Britney to do certain things as her career progressed, but some go back farther. They want to know why I said yes to that little girl with the big, brown eyes and ribbons in her hair when she begged me to take her to the next dance recital and the competition after that one.

> WHAT I DIDN'T KNOW THEN WAS EXACTLY WHAT HER DREAM WAS: TO BECOME A POP STAR LIKE MADONNA OR MARIAH CAREY OR WHITNEY HOUSTON.

That's easy. I said yes to local competitions and then to trying out for the *Mickey Mouse Club* and then to *Star Search* and the rest because I wanted to help my daughter make her dream come true. What I didn't know then was exactly what her dream was: to become a pop star like Madonna or Mariah Carey or Whitney Houston. She never said this out loud, though, even to me, because it seemed like an impossible wish, coming from where we came from.

Britney always worked hard, entirely on her own initiative, to reach higher notes or dance her routine more gracefully. Why wouldn't I do what I could—within reason—to facilitate her progress?

So I did say yes, to a point. If we could help her by driving her to something and taking the time to wait for her and encourage her and watch her as she performed, we would. Of course our family had jobs and school and church and other things that took priority, but Jamie and I wanted to help our child along the way, just like any parents who have driven hours to a soccer tournament and sacrificed their own weekend plans over and over again for a child. You tell me, what's the difference? I sure wish I knew. In any other arena of competition—academics, sports, you name it—if a mother carpools and waits for hours, or—*heaven forbid*—voices concern about the teaching or coaching her child receives, she is an attentive, active parent. But if you take your child to a talent competition or to an audition for a TV show, there's a completely different vibe. And when your child actually excels in acting or singing or dancing—watch out. If you utter a peep of dissent or stick up for your child in any way, you'll have the label "stage mom" slapped on you so fast it'll make you dizzy. That label, my friend, is glued on with heavy-duty epoxy that no solvent on this earth can dissolve.

Maybe this would be a good time to mention that I have never been a manager for either of the girls, although I was paid for a time to work on Britney's fan club and Web site. And, believe it or not, I was never paid a penny for exclusive interview deals with magazines or anything like that—ever.

But let's get back to my real role: Britney's mom, who did agree most of the time to help her determined little girl reach for the stars.

One thing it was harder to say yes to was the biggest trip we took to Atlanta, when Britney was about nine, to try out for the *Mickey Mouse Club* show. It was around an eight-hour drive, and I was eight months pregnant with Jamie Lynn, roly-poly, awkward, and very uncomfortable.

We made it in one piece without me going into early labor, and Britney auditioned in front of casting director Matt Casella, who discovered such Hollywood heavy hitters as Ryan Gosling and Keri Russell. Britney sang "Sweet Georgia Brown" and threw in some flips from her gymnastics days and some dance moves as well. More than two thousand children auditioned, but Matt knew right away that both Britney and a girl named Christina Aguilera from Pittsburgh, also nine, had something special. Both girls were too young at the time to be on the show, but Matt told me and Christina's mother that the girls should try out again in a couple of years. He would be watching for us.

Matt is a wonderful person and a friend to this day. He gave Britney's name to an agent in New York, the lovely Nancy Carson. Nancy suggested we send some footage of Britney to her office. In the video we sent, Britney was singing "Shine On, Harvest Moon," an old-fashioned tune that displayed the power and versatility of her voice. Nancy noted right away that she was struck by the maturity and depth of Britney's vocals for someone that young. We traveled as a family to New York by train to meet with Nancy, and she suggested Britney take some vocal and acting classes at the Professional Performing Arts School in the city, in addition to regular classes. After Jamie Lynn was born, the three of us girls—me, Britney, and Jamie Lynn—sublet an apartment, and we ended up staying in New York for four months after Britney won the part of Laura Bundy's understudy in the off-Broadway production of *Ruthless! The Musical.* It was a spoof of the big Broadway musicals, such as *Mame* and *Gypsy*, and debuted off-Broadway on March 13, 1992. It closed January 24, 1993, after 342 performances.

I know it sounds strange coming from a Southern, rural girl who can't stop singing the praises of small-town life, but I loved New York City and its electric energy, and I still do. All my senses were heightened by the lights and the ceaseless hustle; the endless stream of people coming and going never fails to invigorate me. But it was a far cry from life in Kentwood, that's for sure.

One incident I'll never forget during our time in New York was a trip we took on the subway one day. Britney and I and baby Jamie Lynn used to get around quite handily on the subway system, once I got the hang of figuring out the schedules. On this particular occasion, like many others, I was uncomfortable around some of the rougher-looking characters on the train. One man especially looked scary, with ragged, dirty clothes, unkempt hair and beard, and a look of dejection hanging on him like a mantle. I actually had been thinking, *That cat's a garbage man by day and a serial killer by night*, when it was time for us to get off the train. I was trying to hoist two-month-old Jamie Lynn's stroller (with her in it) from the train to the platform, and the stroller got stuck in the door. Britney and I started tugging at it, our efforts becoming more desperate as the seconds clicked away. We knew that we had mere moments before the train would start moving, and if we didn't get the stroller untangled, the train would drag the stroller, baby and all, along with it. This was literally a life-or-death situation.

The really ironic part is that the businessmen in designer suits just watched us struggle, and not one of them lifted a finger to help. Suddenly, the "serial killer," who was on the platform by then, jumped to our aid and quickly jerked the stroller free. Britney and I were crying at that point, horrified by our experience. But when I turned to thank the man for likely saving Jamie Lynn's life—and probably mine, too, as I would never have let

> WE HAD MERE MOMENTS BEFORE THE TRAIN WOULD START MOVING, AND IF WE DIDN'T GET THE STROLLER UNTANGLED, THE TRAIN WOULD DRAG THE STROLLER, BABY AND ALL, ALONG WITH IT. THIS WAS LITERALLY A LIFE-OR-DEATH SITUATION.

go of that stroller—he was gone. He had literally vanished within seconds. To this day, I believe he was some kind of angel.

Usually, our everyday life in New York was far more mundane. The three of us would get up early in our little sublet apartment on Forty-eighth Street, and Britney would attend classes at the Professional Performing Arts School. After school, we would go to the theater, where Britney would rehearse her lines. As an understudy, she wasn't on most nights, but on a few different occasions she had to perform. Natalie Portman was the other understudy for the main role of Tina Denmark; Laura Bell Bundy played Tina in the lead role.

It would make for long days and late nights. I also missed Bryan, who was fourteen at the time, so much. He and I would talk by phone daily, and though I worried about him, I felt that he was in good hands with his daddy, who wasn't drinking at the time—or so I thought. Turns out Jamie did start drinking again heavily during those few months, but I didn't find out about it until we were safely at home in Kentwood. Our marriage was already fragile, but my absences—first to New York and later to Orlando—didn't contribute to our split as much as one might think. For most of our life together, Jamie was the one off on a job some-where, not me. And to be honest, I was relieved to escape the tension and the drinking. The main concern for me was that Bryan was being taken care of. Besides Jamie, there was a whole infrastructure of friends, family, and neighbors who kept an eye on Bryan during this time. Our dear neighbors, the Reeds, also had children at Parklane Academy, Bryan's school, and would shuttle him to his sports events when Jamie couldn't. Plus, my best friend, Jill, was Jamie's secretary at this time and she worked out of our home. Bryan seemed fine, but that didn't mean I didn't feel torn. It was the first—but not nearly the last—time I wanted badly to be in two places at one time.

After a few months, it was Christmastime, and while Britney had a great time working on the show up until then, she was starting to show signs of homesickness and fatigue, and so were we all. Rehearsal would start at two o'clock, and she would have to stay through the performance. Sometimes, we wouldn't get home until past midnight. As Christmas approached, she became more and more homesick. She was slated to perform on Christmas Day, and that was a tough call for a little girl, even a born performer like Britney. Then Bryan called, and I could sense the strain in his voice and how much he wanted us to come home. That did it. Show or no show, something had to give. I went to Nancy and told her we were all struggling with staying in New York, especially Britney. She was wonderful, immediately reassuring me that she would worry about getting Britney out of the contract and that we should definitely do what was best for our family and go home.

"Mama, can we go home?" my daughter tiredly asked me, that very day. After four months in New York, it was time to go back to Louisiana. And once again, I said yes.

fourteen

MAMA

At first, Mama did not understand why I was helping Britney achieve her dreams, running myself ragged working all day and turning around and shuttling her to team dance in New Orleans or a competition in Lafayette or where have you.

Mama was from a different era, one where people's children just did not compete in talent competitions, and one where, certainly, you didn't move yourself and part of your family halfway across the country so your ten-year-old could perform in a play. It was a foreign concept to her, just as it was to many of the people in our community who had never in their lives dreamed of doing something so outrageous.

It was foreign to me, too, truth be told, a brave new world I didn't quite understand or trust. If I had ambitions for Britney, it wasn't that she would be a pop star. That would have been about as realistic as me planning for her to become a princess! It never even occurred to me that it was possible. But I did think she had a shot at Broadway, especially after winning that role in *Ruthless!* Before New York, though, my hopes for her were quite down-to-earth. I imagined her being a TV newscaster someday, something that was feasible in our small-town Louisiana world.

Mama had her misgivings at first, but she was always proud of her granddaughter's talents in singing and dancing. "You loved to sing and dance all the time," she told me. "It must be in Britney's genes. Music runs in our blood." She liked to remember her Aunt Nip and Uncle Desmond's household in England, where family members were always singing and dancing and playing music.

Though Mama was already ailing, she came to visit us in New York for a week, and she adored every minute of the hustle and bustle, which reminded her of London. Though her eyes were shining as we took in the bright lights of the big city, I could tell Mama was slowing down considerably. Somehow I knew time was running out for us, but thankfully, I didn't know how close we were to the end.

Gone for Good

At the tender age of twenty-eight, Mama had been diagnosed with rheumatoid arthritis. For a farmer's wife with three young children, this was a terrible blow, yet she always coped with it stoically. She had pain and swelling in her joints, and I would catch her rubbing her hand or her neck often throughout her busy day. At the time, her doctors prescribed cortisone, a steroid hormone, to treat the disorder; it was a course of therapy that over time became more threatening than the illness itself. Back then, this was the remedy of choice for most arthritis patients—and most people trusted their doctors implicitly. What we know now, after many years of seeing the harmful effects of too much cortisone, is that it can cause all kinds of problems, and in Mama's case, the drugs made her bones brittle and paper-thin.

Just fifty-four when she was widowed, Mama's arthritis worsened after Daddy died. She endured terrible pain in her back, especially during any kind of seasonal shift, yet she continued to come help me at my day care every day. When I look back at that window of time, with me, my sister, and my mother working together almost daily, I cherish those days. We laughed a lot, which took Mama's mind off the nagging pain in her body. But as she got well into her fifties and then her sixties, the suffering was becoming disabling. Her doctors suggested she have surgery to relieve some of the constant pressure in her back, and Mama agreed.

While under general anesthetic—for too lengthy a time, my siblings and I believed—Mama suffered a series of small strokes. The doctor later confirmed this was true. Though I was worried about her during her surgery, I had no idea she would come out of it with some of her functioning altered for good. When she woke up, her face was monstrously distended and bloated, and though I was horrified to see my beautiful mother in that condition, I had something even more pressing on my mind right then: I was in labor with Jamie Lynn.

The physical manifestations of Mama's strokes would disappear quickly; in the long term, she had no drooping facial features or any of the other usual signs of stroke. But Mama had changed; there was no doubt about it. Her memory, for one, was affected, and she could no longer pay attention to reading her beloved books. Though she was able to visit us in New York several months after the operation, it was clear she wasn't the same woman she once was. That person, sadly, was already gone for good.

The Earth Cracks Open

After Britney had made the cut for *The Mickey Mouse Club*, and we had only been in Florida—where they taped the show—for two weeks, I got the call I had been dreading for years. Jamie was the one who told me that the earth—my earth—had cracked open again, just as it had fifteen years ago when Daddy had been in that accident with the milk truck.

"Lynne, what are you doing right now?" I could tell from the tone of his voice something awful had happened. "I have some bad news for you. Who's with you right now?" My first thought was Bryan, who had so many close calls over the years. *Please God, don't let it be Bryan.*

And then he told me Mama had died in Sonny's swimming pool. My young nephew had been in the pool with her, and he noticed that his grandma was facedown in the water. At first he thought she was just floating, but he quickly realized something was drastically wrong. He called my brother, his uncle, in from the barn and said to come quick, that something was wrong with Grandma.

Sonny found her dead, of what cause he didn't know. Actually, none of us will ever know if she died of a seizure or another stroke, or what really caused her heart to stop beating. Sonny decided against an autopsy because he figured it would do no good. She was gone.

Needless to say, I was torn to pieces. Not only had I not been able to say good-bye to my mama, but there we were, in a strange place, far from home and family. We couldn't even afford airfare home for the funeral, but God sent a Good Samaritan in the form of Lynn Harless, my new friend and the mother of one of Britney's cast mates, Justin Timberlake. She lent us the money to fly home right away, and I will always be grateful for that.

Though I was shattered by Mama's death, I took great comfort in listening to people's stories at Mama's memorial service. It sounds a bit strange, maybe, but she had the funniest funeral! I laughed through tears all the way through, as folks celebrated her life by telling some great stories. Her pastor, for example, told how he had come to visit her one day and found Mama—a highly modest Methodist lady, remember!—in a state of undress that shocked both of them. You see, in those days she lived out on the dairy farm pretty much by herself, and that farm is in the sticks. I mean, even her mailbox was down the road a ways. So nobody could blame her for washing her car one sticky, hot Louisiana summer day in her skivvies! The poor thing was mortified, though, when the pastor's car drove up into plain sight: she could see him plain as day, and he had a crystal-clear view of her standing there in her bra and undies. "Oh! Oh! *Wait!*" she had called out, in her high, feminine British accent, before making a mad dash for the house.

Jamie also recounted one of mama's quirky habits in the kitchen. "Miss Lillian cooked every Sunday, and it didn't matter if it was four people or twenty people, she would only open *one* can of green peas," he said. "Of course now, Sonny always got served first, and she made sure Sonny had a nice helping of peas on his plate!" Jamie still loves to tell this story! My brother was special to our mother. Not only was he the only boy, but he also ran the dairy and would come to have coffee with Mama every morning. They had a wonderful, close-knit bond.

After the whirlwind of the funeral and all the visitors died down, we returned to Florida, where I really started feeling the aching void my mother's death had left in my life. Still, I couldn't let my children see how much pain I was in. I did most of my grieving in private moments, when the girls were asleep at night. During the days, I hid my mourning and went about my business. After all, as an alcoholic's wife, I had learned well how to put a good face on things, no matter what was happening. But I was shaken to the core, which revealed itself in interesting ways.

I have a theory that when you miss someone, you may find yourself imitating that person. I found myself copying Mama more in the weeks and months after her death by loving up extra on my kids, keeping a meticulous house, and dressing my children the way she would have done, neat as a pin. I even ironed more than usual. Thank goodness that particular manifestation of bereavement didn't last too long!

You may think it's odd, but there was one consoling thought that eventually broke through my fog of grief, a thought that gives me comfort to this day: both Mama and Daddy died doing what they loved.

Daddy was driving, and Mama was swimming. Somehow I can picture them both doing just those things now, on the other side.

fifteen

Mouseketeer Days

All of Kentwood were glued to their TVs on the night Britney competed on *Star Search*. Later, when she was on the Disney Channel for *The All New Mickey Mouse Club,* it seemed as though half the town modernized and got cable so they could watch her!

Britney had tried out for the pre–*American Idol* singing competition while we were in New York, and she was excited to be on national television, competing with the nation's top young singers. When it was time for her to compete, she won the first round but lost the next time around. She sang "Love Can Build a Bridge," by the Judds, and the power of the lyrics matched the depth and power of Britney's ten-year-old voice. She did not like to lose one little bit, and though it was painful, the fighter in her would not allow herself to feel defeated.

As I said, back in Kentwood we had tons of support and encouragement from our community. People were so proud of the little girl they could call one of their own.

But then there was also another, much smaller group of folks back home—those who thought we were crazy. Well, they thought I was crazy, anyway. They would say, "Who do you and your daughter think you are? No one around here has ever done anything like this before."

The truth is, I didn't think much about Britney's future, if at all. My child had already realized her dreams in such an amazing way, what could possibly top being on national television? I simply did not have the huge ambitions for her that I have been accused of having. If a door opened, we walked through it.

> I SIMPLY DID NOT HAVE THE HUGE AMBITIONS FOR HER THAT I HAVE BEEN ACCUSED OF HAVING. IF A DOOR OPENED, WE WALKED THROUGH IT.

Yet there was no denying Britney's innate desire to perform—on the playground, in church, in the shower—she sang to the rooftops every day, with absolutely no prodding from me.

Does a bird need a nudge from its mother to sing? Britney sang from the depths of her young being, because I believe that's what she was meant to do. I felt that by shutting the doors that were opening to her, I would be locking down something essential and primal inside of her. In the end, I would not put a cage around that bird.

Justin and the Mouseketeers

Christina Aguilera & Britney backstage at the Mickey Mouse Club.

When she was eleven, going on twelve, Britney auditioned again for *The Mickey Mouse Club*. There were three intense days in the tryout camp to become a Mouseketeer, and it all boiled down to a five-minute audition, where each child was supposed to sing two songs, dance, and perform a comedy monologue.

The second time was a charm for both Britney and Christina: both girls made it as cast members on *MMC*, as it was generally known. Ryan Gosling,

84

Barney and Lillian Bridges—a wartime romance.

One of three or four baby pictures
of me—a rarity.

Me in the sixth grade

Sandra, the happy bride, with her miserable family in those uncomfortable clothes.

Jamie was best man at his brother Austin's wedding. Britney was the flower girl and Bryan was the ring bearer.

Bryan, my little soldier.

Britney strikes a pose as we are getting
ready to go to church for Easter Sunday.

At our neighbor Cindy Reed Miller's wedding; Bryan was an usher, Jamie Lynn was a flower girl, and Britney sang the same song she would later showcase at Jive Records.

Sonny's wedding; Sandra and I were so happy when Sonny found Wanda.

I'm biased, but Jamie Lynn was the most scrumptious little girl in the world.

Bryan and Sandra adored each other.

A yearbook photo of Britney and Justin with my second-grade class.

who has become a big movie star in such films as *The Notebook*, and Justin Timberlake were also on the show at that time. My first impression of the biggest pop stars in the world? I just thought they were sweet kids! JC

> MY FIRST IMPRESSION OF THE BIGGEST POP STARS IN THE WORLD? I JUST THOUGHT THEY WERE SWEET KIDS!

Chasez, a future member of *NSYNC, and actress Keri Russell were also cast members during Britney's era.

Justin

One day when Britney was about thirteen and Jamie Lynn was just a toddler, we all went to a local pastor we knew for some family counseling. Jamie's drinking had been out of control, and I thought this pastor could give us some much-needed guidance on how to keep us four from splintering. We only went a few times—nobody except me really appreciated what the pastor was saying—but he did point out something profound. "If this young lady [Britney] and her daddy don't resolve their issues, and he doesn't try harder to establish a good, strong relationship with her, she will end up clinging to the first real romance in her life. That man will be of extreme importance in her life, and that relationship will determine the course of all her relationships with men from then on."

I couldn't know it at the time, but of course, the first true romance in Britney's life was Justin, her childhood sweetheart, the one who had been friends with her since they were both young cast mates on *MMC*. His mother was my good friend, and we watched them grow up together. Later we would also watch them rise in fame together. From his days on *MMC*, to *NSYNC, to branching out in his own incredibly successful solo career, Justin and Britney followed a very similar trajectory to superstardom. Lynn Harless and I would truly have a front row seat, the two of us mothers watching in awe as our children became the world's biggest pop stars.

J. C. Chasez, Britney, Justin, and I when Britney was opening for *NSYNC.

Britney and Justin started dating when she was eighteen. They were a lot alike, those two—much more so than Britney and her future husband, Kevin, would be alike. Perhaps Justin and Britney were too similar and butted their strong wills together too often. For the most part, I liked their relationship, although not every aspect of it was pleasing to me. Early in their relationship, for example, she and Justin had been having heartfelt conversations about the meaning of life, as all young adults do, and one day she came to talk to me.

"Mama, I just don't know if there really is a right and a wrong anymore," she said thoughtfully. "I mean, is anything really *wrong*?" Looking back, that's about the time Britney started questioning her Christian faith. I do believe she will come back to her faith roots someday soon, but this was really where she took a left turn on her spiritual journey. In a way, I understood, remembering how I had doubts myself in my world religion class at my Catholic high school.

And I didn't like it one bit, later on, that the two of them were going to buy a house and live together, at the age of nineteen. But at that point, I could have talked until I was blue in the face about morals and values and—for heaven's sake—good common sense! No one was particularly open to my input at that time; let's put it that way.

Justin was part of our family for four years, and to me he will always be that cute, sweet kid from our *Mickey Mouse Club* days. Justin and Britney's breakup, though, would be a terrible thing for all involved. I wish they would have parted ways differently, rather than to hurt each other and leave all those scars. It was a story with no end, or rather, I should say, it was a story with two endings, one made up by Britney and one by Justin—it wasn't healthy for either of them. But that was all to unravel in the far future. For us, Florida was a gateway to a whole new way of life.

> JUSTIN WAS PART OF OUR FAMILY FOR FOUR YEARS, AND TO ME HE WILL ALWAYS BE THAT CUTE, SWEET KID FROM OUR *MICKEY MOUSE CLUB* DAYS.

Orlando

The day we left for Orlando, practically the whole town of Kentwood turned up to send us off to Florida, where *The Mickey Mouse Club* taped. There was a huge cake, and they declared it Official Britney Spears Day. Britney and I were both overwhelmed at the kindness and warmth of the well-wishers from our town.

Christina, Justin, and Ryan and their mothers lived in the same apartment complex as Britney, Jamie Lynn, and I, and we all became good friends. For two years in a row, for four months at a time, the other moms and I bonded at the pool, going shopping, going out to eat, and hanging out at Disney World, where we all had complete access because of our affiliation with Disney. As opposed to later years, when Jamie Lynn was taping *Zoey 101,* Disney didn't want the parents on the set at all except during the two days when the show was taped. This meant toddler Jamie Lynn and I had plenty of time on our hands. I'd cook, clean, and basically fulfill my general routine as a mom, and we'd go to the pool or play at Disney World. Friends such as Margaret would come and visit and take advantage of the all-access pass we had to the theme park. Not bad as perks go.

In no time, Christina and Britney were thick as thieves. Christina has the sweetest mom, who has a heart of gold. She was full of creativity and ideas and love for her daughter. But you know teenagers. They think the grass is always greener at their friends' houses. Christina was over all the time for meals and for sleepovers. I think she was drawn to my Southern cooking, and she really was like another daughter for a while. I am so proud of that girl and the woman she has become!

The show was an absolutely terrific training ground for these stars in the making. They learned to sing and dance and act and do sketch comedy. Those *Mickey Mouse Club* numbers groomed Britney to be a pop star, although at the time I never could have imagined what her future held. We were just taking things one opportunity at a time.

Christina and Britney cried their eyes out when the show ended after two seasons. They had so much in common and had become such close friends. *MMC* had become like a family for all of us, and the show itself was a nurturing place to develop their skills. It was hard to see that era end, but, on the other hand, it was time again to go back home to Louisiana.

Normal Girl

We returned to Kentwood, where Britney just wanted to go back to being a regular kid: play basketball, go to school, do all those "normal" things she had missed out on. Or at least that's what she thought she wanted.

I was as happy as a clam to get back into my routines at home of cooking, gardening, shuttling kids around to various places. Truly, home in my small town is my natural habitat, where I feel the most comfortable, settled, and content. Then one day Britney came and talked with me. She wasn't nearly as content as I was to live the everyday life back home. "I want to sing, Mom," she said. "I would like to be homeschooled."

Wow. One day your kid wakes up and announces she wants something completely different for her life than you thought she did. Or at least, she wanted that something faster than I thought she would. I assumed she would finish out her schooling in Kentwood and then pursue a career in entertainment. Instead she wanted to be homeschooled so she could get on with singing—now.

"But honey, I thought you were so happy in school!" was the first thing that popped out of my mouth. Her declaration, so earnest and genuine, came out of the blue for me, although in retrospect I should not have been so shocked. The showbiz bug had bitten my girl hard. We had a decision to make: would we help our daughter achieve her dreams now, or would we make her wait until she was an adult and could strike out on her own? Jamie was 100 percent on board with the former. He wanted his daughter to succeed, and many times he would find a way to make it happen. When we didn't have money to travel to an audition, Jamie would often pull it out of a hat somehow, borrowing it from friends and paying them back as soon as he was able. In terms of Britney and her dreams, he never left her stranded. My opinion? We would take it one opportunity at a time, just as we always had.

That next summer, when Britney was fourteen, a friend had heard about an audition in New York for an all-girl band. I was teaching, and we couldn't afford airfare for me anyway; how would we get Britney to New York? Once again, my friend Margaret saved the day, traveling with

Britney to the audition and paying for her own airfare and expenses as well as some of Britney's expenses. They stayed with friends of ours from the *Ruthless!* days.

The contact in New York was a creep; Britney and Margaret both felt that right off the bat. He could not be trusted to keep his word on anything, although he was full of promises. Britney knew immediately she did not want to work with him, but one good thing came out of that contact: he introduced us to Larry Rudolph, an entertainment lawyer who became Britney's trusted agent for many years. First, though, we started by asking Larry for advice.

I sent him a recent photo of Britney, an Instamatic picture I had taken of her. A photographer I am not, but evidently the photo was clear enough to show him how beautiful Britney was. "Send me a tape of her singing," he said.

I mailed Larry a tape of Britney singing at a wedding soon after that. "We may have something here," was his response. Then he sent her a song that had been rejected for one of Toni Braxton's albums, and Britney recorded it. On the strength of that song, he was able to arrange for a meeting in New York with a couple of record labels.

At the time, we certainly didn't have the money to fly ourselves to New York. It was a slow time period for Jamie's construction business, and we were still in the gutter financially, owing more than we were earning. The two hundred dollars per ticket might as well have been two *thousand* dollars a ticket. Larry paid for that trip to New York, or we never would have gone. In the days and weeks preceding the audition, we were guardedly excited; after all, what good does it do to get ahead of yourself? We had no idea what would happen in New York.

For her audition at Jive Records, they asked Britney to sing something a cappella, which she was not prepared for. I suggested she sing Whitney Houston's version of one of our favorite hymns, "Amazing Grace." At the time, her Christian walk was so strong, and she sang that great hymn of the faith with all the heartfelt emotion in the world, adding all kinds of runs and bells and whistles. That song blew away the fifteen men in suits sitting in that office. I prayed for her the whole time because it was such an intimidating situation, and we were both feeling anxious. But when she started singing that ageless song with such clarity and beauty, she sounded astonishing, like a young Aretha Franklin, soulful and pure. In my mind that's what her "real" voice sounds like, a wholesome, powerful sound, not like the breathy, super-produced pop voice given to her by record producers. She had her "showcase," or audition, at Mercury Records the next day.

> IN MY MIND THAT'S WHAT HER "REAL" VOICE SOUNDS LIKE, A WHOLESOME, POWERFUL SOUND, NOT LIKE THE BREATHY, SUPER-PRODUCED POP VOICE GIVEN TO HER BY RECORD PRODUCERS.

Mercury passed on her.

"I just don't see it," an executive over there told Larry. (I'll bet he "sees it" now!) Thankfully, Jive had a completely different response, a clear yes to this young teen and her powerful voice. They signed her to a recording contract. From that moment on, Britney's life has been on a course not unlike a race track—fast, exhilarating, and full of twists and turns both exciting and dangerous. More than once in the next few years, my precious child would hit the wall, and the impact would have painful reverberations for every member of my family.

This is coming from a mother's heart, not a professional record executive, but before the recording studios tinkered with that big, bold voice, my sweet girl could blow the roof off a house with her strength and passion. My prayer for Britney, then and now, is that she regains her once strong, true voice again, in more ways than one.

sixteen

FIRST TASTE OF FAME

When Britney left home for the first time, I felt a deep pit in my stomach.

As a fifteen-year-old, she had been signed by Jive to a developmental deal, and when she was just sixteen, the record company sent her to New Jersey first, and then Sweden, to work with writer-producer Max Martin, who had helped create hits for the Backstreet Boys and Ace of Base.

I was teaching at the time, and Jamie Lynn was just in kindergarten. I couldn't leave my responsibilities at home, so I allowed Britney to travel with a dear friend of mine, Felicia Culotta, a young woman who worked alongside my best friend, Jill, as a dental hygienist in Kentwood.

I look back now and think the dread I felt was a combination of things—the wrenching a mother feels when her child leaves the nest for the first time; the conflicted desire to be with both of my daughters at the same time, even though I knew Jamie Lynn needed me more; and mostly, the fear of the unknown.

When my precious child walked through that doorway, what would be on the other side?

I convinced myself that this was what Britney had dreamed of since she was a tiny girl; *this* was what she had been begging me to help her achieve since those early days of dance recitals and talent competitions, even though Lord knows I had no idea we would ever get this far. God had opened door after door, which seemed to indicate that it was his will for her to walk through them. I still believe he meant for her to do just that. Of course, our choices on the other sides of those open doors have everything to do with making the most—or not—of the opportunities we are given. And unfortunately, as the business got bigger and seemed to take over more and more of Britney's life, we as parents started to lose sight of the choices being made. Yet, that was down the road a ways. We still had no idea that one day soon, the more money she made, the less influence we would have over our own child. In fact, within a year, what we thought didn't amount to a hill of beans to Britney.

But before the tornado of fame blew through our lives, we had plenty to worry about at home. Finances were extremely tight, and my marriage was hanging by a string. I was driving Grandma Lexie's old jalopy, and we barely had enough money to keep the lights on. The phone was already turned off, due in large part to one of Jamie's workers, who had stolen his cell phone and rung up twelve hundred dollars in calls. Before we were able to resolve the matter with the phone company, they turned off all our phone access, including our home phone.

I remember when Britney had just come home from Europe, and I was planning a birthday party for Jamie Lynn, who was about to turn six. She was so excited about her party, and I wanted to make it special for her. Jamie had promised to come home from his job (he was still on the road a lot with his construction jobs) and cook for the event, which meant the food would be outstanding. I'm sure I bored my friends and coworkers half to death with my daily updates on the party—who was coming, what cute decorations we would have, and what kinds of foods we would eat. Every person in that lunchroom knew *way* too much about that party and had patiently answered questions from me like, "Do you think this type of potato salad will go with that kind of meat?" "What kind of punch do you think—Orange Splash or Red Berry Zing?" In hindsight, clearly this obsession with my little girl's party was my way of distracting myself from our family's troubles.

Then one day, as the party got closer, something happened that disallowed me to pretend anymore. I was sitting in the lunchroom with Joy, eating, when someone said I had a call in the office. When I returned, Joy says the look on my face was wretched.

"Jamie's not coming home for the party," I said, bursting into tears. "Jamie Lynn will be heartbroken!"

Then I remembered something: I hadn't ever told Jamie Lynn her daddy would be cooking for her party. Had something deep down told me she might be disappointed? After a few minutes of feeling sorry for myself, I pulled it together; it was back to the drawing board. My wonderful principal, Charlie Schwartz, gave me his calling card—not for the first or last time—to make calls (remember, our phone was disconnected) to come up with a plan B for food. We ate hot dogs, potato salad, chips and dip—simple kids' party food, and Jamie Lynn had a ball. She never even knew her daddy had copped out, which was the way I wanted it. Still, disillusionments and money pressures were piling up. How soon would it be before our house of cards collapsed?

The Calm Before the Storm

When Britney was in Sweden recording her first album, life as we knew it back home was pretty much the same. We were thrilled that Britney was realizing her dream of making a record, but our day-to-day lives had yet to change. When she left, Britney and I both cried our eyes out, and we had tearful long-distance phone calls, each of us taking turns telling the other how much she was missed. Sometimes we talked up to eight times a day! I missed my daughter dreadfully, but there was a silver lining: Britney was being given the opportunity to do what she had always wanted to do.

Felicia was and is so sweet and bubbly, and she had the diligence and responsibility, we felt, to be the adult figure when we could not. We couldn't be in Sweden and Louisiana, so Felicia was our good, honest person in charge, the one with the discernment to assess all the different people our teenage daughter was coming in contact with.

After a few months in Europe, Britney came home to an overjoyed mother and family. The first record would not release until January 1999—a good eight months from then—but Jive already had their marketing machine operating at full throttle. The first single, ". . . Baby One More Time," would air in October, and that summer Jive arranged for Britney to do a tour of twenty-six shopping malls all over the country. They set up a Web site and sent out hundreds of thousands of postcards. The excitement was building!

Jamie Lynn and I traveled with Britney somewhat during that summer, but I had bigger fish to fry at home; Felicia stepped in again to be with Britney. In July, Jamie and I filed for bankruptcy after years of financial trouble. We had to close down Jamie's spa/gym—Total Fitness, the one that we had opened during the "golden years." Because he was working on construction jobs in Jackson or Memphis, he couldn't oversee it well, and we could no longer pay our employees properly, although we made sure to pay them before our creditors. Four years before, in 1994, we, along with two business partners, had defaulted on a fifty-three thousand-dollar mortgage for some land we owned near our home. The property was seized by the Tangipahoa Parish sheriff and auctioned off the following year. I was humiliated, but that wasn't the end of the nightmare. In October 1997, the sheriff returned to haul off our 1993 Ford Probe when it was at the body shop—we still owed more than ten thousand dollars to Ford Motor Company. We were miserable, and we were advised that bankruptcy was our only option.

> NOTHING COULD HAVE
> SAVED US FROM THE
> FINANCIAL CANYON WE HAD
> GOTTEN OURSELVES INTO,
> AND CERTAINLY BRITNEY
> COULDN'T SAVE US, NOR
> DID WE WANT HER TO.

Nothing could have saved us from the financial canyon we had gotten ourselves into, and certainly Britney couldn't save us, nor did we want her to.

Much has been written in the media about how we were counting on our teenage daughter and her singing career to rescue us from financial ruin. "Betting on a horse" and "putting all their eggs in one basket" are just two ways our "strategy" has been described in the press. Ha! When I think of our actual mind-set during those days, that idea is almost laughable.

First of all, Jamie and I had no idea whatsoever that Britney would have a hit record. All she had was a developmental deal with Jive, which was very little money up front, less than five hundred dollars, if I recall correctly, and that was all hers. In a demo deal, a record company sees potential in an artist but is not willing to sign him or her to a full-scale recording contract. It was still very exciting, because even a demo deal is hard to get in the competitive music industry and it could lead to a "real" contract. After Britney taped her demos, Jive would decide for sure if they wanted to sign her. We were told to be prepared for them to possibly pass because, after all, talented singers with demo deals were a dime a dozen in the eyes of the record label. While we hoped and prayed they would sign her, we truly had no idea.

More important, we never felt for a moment that it was our child's responsibility to dig us out of that financial grave. Contrary to popular belief, we never wanted to ride on Britney's coattails, nor did we even know at the time that she would have any "coattails," so to speak, to ride on!

In the summer of 1998, as Britney was hopping from mall to mall, singing and dancing and doing what she had loved all her life, we were happy for her, despite our money nightmares. It was the one bright spot in our lives during that difficult time. We looked ahead to the fall, when Jive would release ". . . Baby, One More Time" on the radio for the first time, and we prayed that the song would somehow notch the Top Forty charts. Even if Britney's single was number forty, the thrill of having our child, who had worked so hard for so long, achieve a top-forty song would last us the rest of our lives.

Of course, we did not have one hot clue what was right around the corner.

seventeen

THE TOUCH OF TIME

Writer Clara Ortega says that with our siblings, we live outside the touch of time. "To the outside world we all grow old," she writes. "But not to brothers and sisters. We know each other as we always were. We know each other's hearts. We share private family jokes. We remember family feuds and secrets, family griefs and joys."

Siblings are our lives' best witnesses, the ones we argued with, who monopolized the bathroom, and who acted as our mirrors, reflecting back to us the whole picture of who we really are, warts and all. They are the bystanders with whom we sat at the dinner table, around the Christmas tree, and through any number of family weddings, graduations, and funerals.

Siblings, I think, are absolutely elemental. No matter how much your brother or sister irritated you, borrowed your clothes and returned them in less-than-stellar condition, or tattled on you to your parents, they are the ones with you cradle to grave.

They are the ones who will defend you to all comers.

When I think of the sibling relationships in my family, so many pictures and stories come to my mind:

- My brother, Sonny, and I taking turns riding Wishbone, our horse, in the pasture.
- Britney gazing in adoration at her baby sister, holding her blanketed bundle with all the care and attention of a mother.
- Sandra sizing up the fact that my family would have little or no gifts under our tree one year, calling up Connie's Jewelers in town and authorizing a five-hundred-dollar line of credit for me to buy Christmas gifts.
- Britney and Jamie Lynn, at ages twenty-two and twelve, wearing Halloween masks and flinging Sonic milk shakes at paparazzi who had gathered in Kentwood after Britney and Kevin got married.
- Preston and Jayden, uncertainty written all over their innocent, baby faces, clasping hands in the backseat of their mama's car as what seemed like a million flashbulbs went off all around them. Though they couldn't articulate it, they were reaching out to each other, offering the comfort and strength of their brotherhood to each other.

I think of Bryan, age seventeen, on one of the numerous occasions he ratted out one of his little sisters. Once it was Britney. When she was thirteen, we had a very old truck, its color something that does not occur in nature. We called it the Green Lizard. Britney and her cousin, Laura Lynne, were learning to drive. Yes, I know, they were thirteen, but this is the rural South we are talking about—wide-open spaces and hardly any traffic to speak of. The girls were limited to their driveways, or maybe just a small piece of road right by their houses. And always, *always* they were to have a parent in the vehicle with them. That was the rule.

One night, the two girls sneaked out of the house and drove around the block in the Green Lizard. We may never have known about that little escapade, were it not for the fact that Bryan was happy to report it to us. Britney was grounded, and her immediate consequence was that she had to clean the yard. I can still see her, stomping around the yard, picking up sticks and things, and shoving them in a bucket, with tears streaming down her face. She was so mad at Bryan!

Bryan may have been gleeful in reporting the incident, but part of his motivation was probably quite good, noble, even. Britney would say a *very* small part. He's always been so protective of Britney and Jamie Lynn.

Though he lives bicoastal for his work, Bryan often knows more about Jamie Lynn and her friends than Jamie and I do. He will call me and tell me what she and her friends are thinking about doing! He's quite the detective when it comes to his sisters. He means well when he tattles, but it's hard for Britney and Jamie Lynn to see it at the time. Their big brother is their greatest defender, as Sandra was mine. I could not imagine my life without her.

Touchstone

My sister, Sandra, was always a touchstone for me, a rock-solid base by which I could measure the goings-on in my own life, no matter how crazy things would get. By 2000, Britney's career had already exploded into something much bigger—and crazier—than any of us ever could have imagined. But at that point, we were still just experiencing the exciting aspects of her success. The drawbacks—unending media scrutiny, stalkers, the plague of paparazzi—had yet to really touch us. It was like a bullet-proof thrill ride—then.

In the midst of that year, though, the dreamlike adventure would be punctured by one devastating piece of news.

Sandra had been experiencing gastrointestinal problems, or so she thought. An ultrasound detected a growth on her ovary that turned out to be malignant. I couldn't believe it. Sandra—my teacher, my defender, my best friend—how could

Sandra and Laura Lynne's first trip to California; we're hanging out at Britney's first house.

she be vulnerable to anything, much less a life-threatening disease? We were both middle-aged women by that point; she was fifty-two, and I was forty-four. Yet, in my mind, she was still that fearless twelve-year-old, watching out for water moccasins down at the creek, with me riding piggyback.

She was the strong one, always. No matter what I was going through with my children or my marriage—anything at all in my life—Sandra would be the person I would turn to for calm, reassurance, and the exact right piece of advice. Not that she was one to spout off unwanted advice—far from it. Sandra always took a good, long time formulating her response to anything. That's how she kept herself so genteel, so beyond reproach. What I mean by that is that Sandra just didn't have the same complications in her life as those of us do—most of us—who don't think before we speak. Sandra never failed to give some thought to a matter before she spoke or acted. As a result, there was a real purity about her conduct and her life that I admired so much.

Her diagnosis shook me to the core, as I was the little sister who always looked to the elder daughter for comfort and sanity in the midst of trouble and pain. Now it was my turn to be tough for Sandra, to try to provide some of the emotional shelter and strength she had always given me.

A snippet from my journal reveals what I was going through at that time: "How can this be? There's too much suffering. How can I keep from going insane?" I railed at God, who gave me such a beautiful, loving sister and seemed to be about to take her away. "How can you allow a wonderful, nurturing, angelic person to endure such heartache and remain whole?" I could only hope that one day I would understand more of his plan, but at the time nothing—especially the providential hand of God—made much sense. Anyone who has experienced the slow decline of a beloved person in her life probably understands what I mean. Nothing rattles your faith like a grim diagnosis for someone you love.

Sandra endured chemo and all the horrible side effects for one year, and then, blessedly, her cancer went into remission. I immediately went into denial, thinking for sure now everything would be as it was, with Sandra the picture of health, and she and I marching through our lives as the indestructible Bridges sisters once more. Or maybe it wasn't denial so much as trying with all my might to hold a positive attitude. Likely, it was a complicated mixture of both.

> ANYONE WHO HAS EXPERIENCED THE SLOW DECLINE OF A BELOVED PERSON IN HER LIFE PROBABLY UNDERSTANDS WHAT I MEAN. NOTHING RATTLES YOUR FAITH LIKE A GRIM DIAGNOSIS FOR SOMEONE YOU LOVE.

We ended up having one year in which I could successfully pretend the cancer would never come back. But it was only a year. Then one day her abdominal pains struck again, until finally she could hardly walk; she was in so much agony.

Sandra had come to visit Britney, and we were all on Melrose Avenue on one of our legendary shopping trips when she doubled over with pain. Ovarian cancer, stealthy, murderous thing that it is, was back, and it never left us again. If you've lost a beloved one to cancer, you know exactly what I mean when I describe those years as a roller coaster I never wanted to get on. For six years, it was a nonstop fight. Her CA 125 blood levels would go up and down. The test wouldn't show much cancer one month, and then the next month her levels would rise again. How I prayed that everything would be okay!

We talked every day at least once, but when I knew she was going in to the doctors for another test, I'd be afraid of her calls. Literally, I'd be so afraid that when the phone rang, I would freeze, paralyzed with fear of what she would say. Was it good news or horrible news?

I ached inside, but I tried to project a positive, cheerful outlook, full of plans for the future that surely Sandra and I would share.

Surely we would, because the alternative was unthinkable.

eighteen

RUDE AWAKENING

Sometimes all you can do is stand there, dazed, and try to make sense of the new reality you must take in. This was my mind-set when ". . . Baby One More Time" debuted at number one on the Billboard 200 charts in the USA. We were all absolutely shell-shocked, no one more so than me.

I mean, who hits it like that the first time out of the gate? I could never have imagined that my little girl would have one of the highest-selling records by a teenager in the history of modern music—and with her first album! All I could do was shake my head in disbelief that this had happened. I knew she was a very talented girl, but *this*? This was stunning. Britney had turned seventeen on December 2, 1998, one month before the album was released.

We were ecstatic for her, of course, but then again I had a job to go to and twenty-some children to teach every day. Jamie Lynn was in first grade, and I remained at home with her while Britney and Felicia roamed all over the world, literally. Life as we knew it was over.

Dazed and Confused

Not everyone who becomes famous does so in a split second. Britney's fame came around the corner, zooming at us at two hundred miles per hour. Ben Affleck is right. He said sudden fame is like being in a car wreck. It comes at you fast, and you spin out of control. But it's a wreck you can walk away from. The injuries come later. Still, you're shook up, dizzy, and in kind of a state of bewilderment about it all. Looking back, it would have been nice to have things evolve a little bit slower, or at least slow enough so we could catch our breath. It took us a while to adjust to the new way of life, with nonstop calls, strangers at our door, and our friends and family also getting deluged. It was absolutely overwhelming.

> SUDDEN FAME IS LIKE BEING IN A CAR WRECK, BUT IT'S A WRECK YOU CAN WALK AWAY FROM. THE INJURIES COME LATER.

In those early days, when Britney's album . . . *Baby, One More Time* had just exploded and Britney was suddenly on television all over the place and in magazines, we didn't even know enough to be afraid of some fans. Southern hospitality runs deep in my bones, and I think I even invited a few folks in to sit a spell and have a glass of sweet tea!

After a few months of this crazy new life, we finally got the clue that not every fan of our daughter was well-intentioned. One incident in particular stands out in my mind. I was home alone one day with Jamie Lynn when we heard pounding on our door. When we peeked around a curtain to see who was on the other side of the door, we saw a stranger, a man who began yelling. "Let me in!" he kept hollering, all the while pummeling the door so hard I thought he might break it right down. I grabbed Jamie Lynn, our cordless phone, and a gun, and we locked ourselves in the bathroom. I quickly called the police, who came within a few minutes and hauled that guy away. We were terrified, and with our hearts hammering in our chests, those minutes seemed to last a lifetime. That's when it first began to dawn on us that we were way too exposed in that house, with no gates or security to speak of.

Jamie Lynn and Crystal used to compete for Big Rob's attention. He's such a fine man.

Soon after the song was a hit, it was decided that Britney needed a bodyguard to protect her from individuals like that man who came to our door. That's when Big Rob came to us, the first of several people God would bring into our lives not only to make us feel safe, but to enrich us all with grace and spiritual strength.

Big Rob was with Britney every waking moment, practically, and he often came to Kentwood and stayed with us. Whenever she would come home, he would come home, and what a delightful man he was. Big Rob was a Christian, and the fact that the man protecting our daughter shared our beliefs was comforting. Funny, sweet, and congenial, that dear man became part of our family. We felt so safe with him around.

He had such a tremendous intuition for things going wrong. One time Britney and I were in New York for some kind of charity event. She was about eighteen then, as this was roughly one year after the album was released.

> BIG ROB WAS A CHRISTIAN, AND THE FACT THAT THE MAN PROTECTING OUR DAUGHTER SHARED OUR BELIEFS WAS COMFORTING.

Big Rob and some other guards were helping us get through a big crowd of people pressing around us to the car. There was a man standing nearby whom I had vaguely noticed, only because he was small in stature, but he had on a big, puffy jacket.

Suddenly, Big Rob lifted Britney and literally threw her in the car. Within two seconds, he also lifted me and threw me in after her. Right before the car door slammed shut, I was dimly aware of a scuffle going on behind the car. Two or three guards were on top of the man in the puffy jacket; he was apparently hiding some box cutters. I don't know what he planned to do with those cutters, or even how Big Rob and those other guards figured out that he had them, but on that occasion and others, his sharp instincts saved the day.

Light-headed

Within a year of the album being released, Britney had won four Billboard Music Awards, including Female Artist of the Year. Keep in mind that fifteen months before that moment, in the fall of 1998, we were praying that her first single would scratch the Top Forty! We were all giddy for Britney and feeling a little light-headed ourselves.

All I knew was that my child had worked very hard, and to see her passion pay off like that was just wonderful. With the release of Britney's second album, *Oops! . . . I Did It Again,* her management team decided she should go on tour. I'm telling you, this all became a huge business before we knew what hit us. With the tour came merchandizing—T-shirts, hats, key chains, and so on—and I was so glad I wasn't ever one of Britney's managers. I would leave it up to the professionals to decide on choreography and key chains, and I would continue teaching my little ones at school

> I WISH NOW I HAD TRUSTED THE PROFESSIONALS A LITTLE LESS AND GIVEN MYSELF MORE CREDIT FOR MY OWN INSTINCTS.

their reading, writing, and arithmetic. Of course, I wish now I had trusted the professionals a little less and given myself more credit for my own instincts.

Britney was sky-high with excitement over it all, and we shared her exhilaration. Still, it was too much to take in sometimes, coming from our normal, workaday world. When Larry and Britney came to me and asked me to quit teaching to travel with her, I was terribly torn. I agonized over that decision, because it would mean leaving behind the career I loved and the still-normal life I felt comfortable in. I'm basically a steady Eddie to my core. I like things to unfold in an orderly, predictable fashion; I was born and bred to expect those things to be true.

Larry pointed out that I could make more income running Britney's fan club part-time than I could teaching full-time, but that didn't really sway me. I loved my students, and I didn't want to leave them. What did finally win me over was the thought that I could keep an eye on things and be with Britney much more. She was only eighteen years old, and she still needed my guidance and influence. I would write a letter for Britney's Web site and do some other things for the fan club. But basically I would be her traveling companion. After much thought—and not, evidently, enough prayer—I decided to quit my job and join my daughter on tour.

Making It

It's hard for me to say exactly how I felt the first time I saw Britney onstage. I was sitting back with the sound guys, a perch that would eventually become my regular place to roost during her shows. Nervousness mingled with excitement and resulted in speechlessness. I watched in awe as Britney sang and danced through her first headlining show. When it was over, I burst into tears, the culmination of an emotionally charged experience capping off years of investment on all our parts to get Britney to this point. Well, I should say, "this point" wasn't exactly anything we could have imagined in our most delusional dreams! But she had achieved far beyond what she had always dreamed of achieving, and as her mother, I applauded that from the depths of my soul. I was so happy for my child. And also a little relieved. Somehow, by the grace of God, mostly, plus years of practice and sweat and tears, she had made it. But at what cost? I was soon to find out that I was in way over my head.

The Rolling Stone *Cover*

The first time I felt my anchor was slipping, that my authority as a mother was really undermined, was Britney's first *Rolling Stone* cover in April 1999. Keep in mind that new things were being flung at us, fast and furious, and I didn't have a hint of what I was doing. I mean, we were straight-off-the-vine ripe, if you know what I mean! *Clueless.* I trusted in the professionals surrounding my daughter to make the right decisions; after all, what did I—a rural Louisiana schoolteacher—know about the music industry? But by deferring to experts, I gave up far too much influence.

The *Rolling Stone* cover was just one of a flurry of new and exciting experiences for Britney—and all of us by extension. Right after . . . *Baby One More Time* hit it so big, the magazine had sent a crew to our old house, a modest brick ranch, to shoot a cover story about Britney. The photographer was an eccentric, artistic guy, and though I thought some of his ideas were strange—rolling our whole house in toilet paper?—I thought he must know what he was doing if he worked for *Rolling Stone.*

Over the course of two days, they shot hundreds of pictures of Britney, outside our house, inside our house, wearing dozens of different outfits. Jamie and I were milling around the house, trying to stay out of the way and peeking in whenever we could to see how the shoot was going. This was our first experience ever with a magazine photo shoot, and we were like deer in the headlights. Britney was exhausted at the end of the second day, and her knee was throbbing.

For some reason (now I know exactly what that reason was), the photographer wanted to shoot some pictures in Britney's bedroom, which was a small room, especially when they had crammed in all of their equipment. No, alarm bells didn't go off in my head—right away. I had no idea the man was going for a lascivious angle. In my still-naive mind, he was going to shoot a sweet picture of a teenage girl in her haven with stuffed animals and posters on the wall and memorabilia on her dresser. Since the room was packed, we couldn't get in there very easily, although Larry did steal a look here and there. When that bedroom door suddenly shut tight, though, alarm bells starting ringing, all right. Larry ducked in to check up on the photographer. When I heard him say, "That's enough," in an unhappy tone, I barged right in after him.

I HAD NO IDEA THE MAN WAS GOING FOR A LASCIVIOUS ANGLE. IN MY STILL-NAIVE MIND, HE WAS GOING TO SHOOT A SWEET PICTURE OF A TEENAGE GIRL IN HER HAVEN.

What I saw was Britney in a bra and hot pants, sitting on her bed. At that moment, I didn't care who was authorizing this photo shoot: it was over. "Let's stop *now*," I said, flustered and uncomfortable. Jamie was furious. "This is stupid!" he said, spitting out his words. He immediately left the house in a huff, not knowing what to do. Still, although we felt the photographer had crossed the line, we were comforted by the fact that no one would ever see a photo of my daughter in that skimpy outfit. Why? We assumed we would have final say over which pictures were chosen. Besides, they took so many cute shots, why would they want this one, taken in her overcrowded little room?

I believe that photographer knew exactly what he was doing, and he also was well aware of the fact that I was never going to be given the right of approval for shots taken of my seventeen-year-old child. And the rub was, I didn't even know enough then to demand to see the shots—I innocently believed the magazine would approach us when they were ready for our opinion! Larry told me recently that in actuality, no one was offered editorial approval, not even him, and since he was also new at this managing business, he didn't realize what would happen either.

When I saw the cover, my heart sank, and my face burned with embarrassment and anger. *Oh my gosh. How did this slip through the cracks? How did this happen?* Already, lines were being crossed. Yet I foolishly thought I was still in control, when in reality my authority was slipping with every day and every dollar being spent—and made—on my daughter's career.

On Tour

Despite that magazine cover—or maybe because of it?—Britney's career exploded, and because I had quit teaching, I joined her on her first world tour in 2000. But as we traveled all over the U.S., Canada, and Europe, our routine was surprisingly dull.

Around noon, Britney would get up (having gotten to bed after midnight, and then sleeping in two shifts), and we would eat, and then she would do her exercises. The afternoon would likely include an interview with a magazine, a newspaper, radio, or TV station, or possibly a charity event of some kind. We would eat supper, and then Britney would have her hair and makeup done. Finally, around eight or nine at night, she would take the stage and perform her show. After unwinding a bit, we would all pile on the bus and sleep until three or four in the morning, when we would be woken up in another city somewhere. We would groggily stumble to our hotel room and sleep until noon, when the whole thing would start all over again.

Actually, it was very boring. If Jamie Lynn was with me, we would do schoolwork together, or if she brought a friend, I would keep an eye on them. She and her friend would have the run of the arena or stadium, and they would bomb around on golf carts, having themselves a big time.

The brightest spot in our day was late at night, after the tour bus had shoved off from whatever city Britney had played in. Jamie Lynn and her friend Crystal would come up with skits and perform them for us all on the bus—but let me tell you, all they cared about was getting a laugh out of Big Rob. Those girls adored the gentle giant who would twirl both of them around his neck at the same time, and they would compete for his attention. In fact, Jamie Lynn came up with Thelma Stump—who would become her signature character on *All That* years later—on that bus. She based her on a mix between her great-grandma Lexie and Big Rob. Crystal was usually Jamie Lynn's straight man, and we would have the best time, night after night, rolling down the highways of the world, laughing ourselves silly.

It was a new kind of routine for us, our "new normal." Interesting, isn't it, how the fantasy of going on a world tour seems to be so glamorous and wonderful, and yet the actuality was fairly monotonous in some ways. But that's fame for you: the way you might imagine it is nothing like the reality. When I first saw big success on its way to my child, I only saw bright lights, fans appreciating her music, and the chance for her to travel and gain a financially secure future. But there are two sides to that coin. When fame turned the corner, if you will, I was in for a rude awakening.

nineteen

CALLING IT QUITS

I never wanted to be alone.

It's almost ironic to say that now, because things have changed so much in the thirty-plus years since Jamie and I got married. When we spoke our vows to each other, those tender, simple words, I could never have imagined for one split second that someday everything would unravel, that in a short period of time I would live each day in uncertainty, never knowing if this was the day the man I loved would act like my husband again.

And that for the better part of the next twenty-four years, he wouldn't act like the man I married.

Divorce was a completely foreign concept to my family. Most of my relatives are still married to their first spouses, including my sister, Sandra, who died after almost four decades of love and commitment to her husband, my brother-in-law, Reggie. Growing up, I never doubted for an instant that I'd get married, live, and die with the man I chose.

But at some point, I "unchose" Jamie Spears.

Some people's marriages end suddenly through the death of a spouse. I can't even begin to imagine how excruciating that loss must be. Others are ambushed by an unexpected conclusion—by affairs and such. My union with Jamie came apart slowly, in sad little pieces.

I'm out on the lawn, trying to throw a football with my strapping, athletic son. No matter how hard I try, I can't throw that ball properly. I know it. Bryan knows it. And all the while we both wish his dad was there instead of me.

Cruel words, flung in the heat of the moment, fueled by alcohol's evil energy. "You're stupid." "You're selfish." "You graduated from college, but you don't even know how to get in out of the rain." And my reactions, so often just as painful. More destructive words, pitched from me to him. The worst part? Knowing my children were hearing every acidic utterance.

Our whole family is in the living room, and Bryan, Britney, and Jamie Lynn are on the couch. I am standing. Jamie is on his hands and knees, crying, pleading. "I love you all so much," he begs. "I am never, never drinking again."

Five years later, when Jamie falls off the wagon again, I can't stop the thought that eats away at me: *Why can't he pull it together now?*

Blame. Guilt. Shame. So much shame. Following the classic co-dependent blueprint, I took on the shame that really belonged to Jamie, or rather, the drinking. So much had transpired in the twenty-four years Jamie and I were married, so many highs and lows that kept me wondering what the next day would bring, endless disappointments that chipped away at my heart and spirit. I had to build wall after wall to survive. The truth is, only so many pieces can break off before there is nothing left of you.

Do You Want to Live Like This?

People always want to know if Britney's fame was the final tipping point that finished off our marriage, and the answer is, obviously, no. There were a thousand sad little pieces, a thousand tipping points. Yes, I traveled quite a bit with Britney, especially when she was in New York doing theater, and then when she was with *The Mickey Mouse Club* in Florida. But by then we had Jamie Lynn, which kept me at home most of the time. The foundation of our marriage was cracked long before Britney began her career as a singer; by the time she became successful, I had already made up my mind to divorce Jamie.

In 2000, eighteen-year-old Britney sat me down. "Mama," she said, "do you want to live like this for the rest of your life?" She meant, of course, did I want to live out my days with a husband who was barely present, never mind supportive or loving? As I said, children of alcoholics are more attuned to the truth of their parents' marriage than anyone else, including the husband and the wife. Britney knew that sometimes, Jamie and I were golden, the sweetest, most loving, most connected couple there was. Only sometimes, though. She also knew that years and years of verbal abuse, abandonment, erratic behavior, and his simply not being there for me had taken their toll. Britney's words echoed the rising sense inside me that my marriage was over. When Jamie found out I was divorcing him, he was irate, of course. Words were said in the heat of anger. Yet there wasn't really much he *could* say; Jamie knew in his heart that this was the toll of his actions over the years. He was angry, but not surprised.

> PEOPLE ALWAYS WANT TO KNOW IF BRITNEY'S FAME WAS THE FINAL TIPPING POINT THAT FINISHED OFF OUR MARRIAGE, AND THE ANSWER IS, OBVIOUSLY, NO. THERE WERE A THOUSAND SAD LITTLE PIECES, A THOUSAND TIPPING POINTS.

Filling the Empty Spaces

I never could have predicted how God would fill up the empty spaces in my life after our divorce. I had always had the strong support of my core group of longtime friends, Jill, Joy, Margaret, and Kelly. They are the kind of friends you call at 3 a.m., as Marlene Dietrich once said. But he also gave me new friends and fresh things to dwell on. Britney was building me a beautiful new house, and I focused on the plans for that. I had been traveling so much with her, and then when we were home, I would devote myself to Jamie Lynn and whatever softball game, basketball game, or gymnastics tournament she was involved in.

You know how, during a complicated, emotional time, you can be so preoccupied with all the mess? That's the way I was for years before my divorce. Half my mind was on my kids and half of it was on Jamie and our marriage. When I finally stopped exerting so much emotional energy into making my marriage work, I threw myself wholeheartedly into my kids.

But I also learned to be alone, and more than that, to relish being so. In my poetry journal from that time period, I poured out all my feelings about the divorce onto paper:

> *Every time I look at you*
> *I see*
> *Bittersweet memories of you and me*
> *Precious moments that we shared from the start*
> *The sad emptiness that pulled us apart*
> *My heart was broken*
> *I built my wall*
> *I'm happy here once and for all*

Looking back, I don't even think "happy" is the right word at all. I would rewrite that now, replacing "happy" with "at peace."

The Bible talks about God being a husband to those who have no husband. Some people might say that passage is referring exclusively to widows, and that may be so. All I know is, God has taken care of me in ways I could never have imagined, carrying me along when I was down and could not walk.

I always feel his protection. Since Britney's first success in 1999, we have had any number of stalkers, deranged individuals who try to get close to my daughters and me. One time, a stalker was living in a collapsed barn right outside our property. He would cut open tin cans with a knife, and he was just waiting for a chance to spot one of us. This guy thought he was married to Britney, who wasn't even living there. Eventually a neighbor spotted him, and the county sheriff arrested him. But even when he was behind bars, this stalker still posed a threat. He had told police that he had planted a bomb on our property, and a bomb squad had to come to our place and search every square inch to make sure there were no explosives.

Things like that have happened, in one way or another, for the last nine years, but I have never really felt afraid. I have two German shepherds who would rip the faces off anyone who would try to hurt me, and of course I have an extraordinary alarm system. And last but not least, I know how to use a gun, and I'm not a bad shot! But my sense of safety goes much deeper than that. Somehow, I feel protected in a divine way that I can't explain.

Standing Alone

Divorce literally means "broken," "detached," "split," and "separated." Each of those words probably jump off the page for those of you who have endured the alienation of someone you once promised to be with forever. Even when a divorce is the only option, there is a grieving process for what could have—and should have—been. After all Jamie and I had been through, I still mourned our lost love and the rare beautiful times we did have. I had to learn to bring each broken piece of my heart to the only one who could mend them. "I'll stand alone," I wrote in my journal during that time. "Lord, guide me today. Hold my hand. Help me find the way."

People ask me why I haven't gotten remarried. I'm no spring chicken, but after all, I am a healthy woman with good teeth and potentially years of life ahead of me! The truth is, I have not even been on one date since I got divorced. No one has even suggested I go on a date with him! I don't know what I would do if a man asked me out. Panic? Stammer? Sometimes I think my rather pathetic lack of a love life is because I am so busy with my children, especially Jamie Lynn, and other times, I wonder if the romantic part of my life is just over. Mainly, I think it is because I am really, truly content to be alone.

twenty

JAMIE LYNN'S TURN

Jamie Lynn has never let many people into her life.

She has a close group of friends, but she also needs her own space. To me, that's a healthy, whole person who doesn't have to be entertained by others all the time. She has always been intensely independent, dressing herself from an early age and completing projects and homework without much help at all from me. Always the teacher, I would have *loved* to help Jamie Lynn with her school projects, but she just never needed it and always managed to make good grades too.

We are very close. But while Britney as a little girl was my shadow, Jamie Lynn has always needed more time alone.

She thinks about everything, and she's so imaginative and creative. Even as a little girl, she was always making up stories and cracking us all up with her fantastic sense of humor, such as how she invented Thelma Stump when she was eight or nine, just to make Britney's bodyguard laugh. To this day, Jamie Lynn can have us all doubled over with one of her famous one-liners.

Thelma Stump, of course, is Jamie Lynn's most fun character so far, an eighty-four-year-old bodyguard who loves bacon. Little did any of us know, back on Britney's tour bus, that Jamie Lynn's impression of Grandma Lexie (and somehow Big Rob too), clomping around with a white wig and a saggy bosom, sniffing out her next hit of bacon, would be the impetus for her own career, separate from her sister's.

Me, Jamie Lynn (as Thelma Stump), Joy, & Leigha backstage at the studio for *All That*.

When Jamie Lynn was ten years old, VH1 did a video spot about Britney that included Bryan and Jamie Lynn rapping and cutting up together. Someone from Nickelodeon saw the video and saw a spark of something special in Jamie Lynn; they called Jive to see if Britney's record company could hook them up with her little sister. Dan Schneider, an executive producer at the network who has been responsible for shows such as *Drake and Josh* and recently *iCarly*, invited Jamie Lynn to come down and audition for *All That*, which was a thrill for her. She had grown up watching the network's version of *Saturday Night Live* or *Mad TV* for kids and had always had an affinity for their brand of off-the-wall humor. One of their funniest sketches featured Amanda Bynes as Meagan Marples, who liked slapping herself with liver! As a little girl, Jamie Lynn loved any comedy sketch with Amanda in it, especially *Whateverrr!*, starring Amanda and Christy Knowlings as Gina and Jessica, a pair of scatterbrained Valley Girls who hosted their own extremely silly, shallow TV show spoof.

Years later, when Jamie Lynn was a regular on the show, she and a fellow cast member would do a take on *Whateverrr!* with their very own sketch called *Trashin' Fashion*, starring as Carly and Marly, two girls with a "passion for trashin' fashion!"

She auditioned for Dan Schneider as Thelma, a feisty old bird with a serious addiction to bacon and an attitude the size of Louisiana. He loved both Jamie Lynn and Thelma, and within a short period of time, he had hired both to mix it up on his show. The setup of the show was similar to *SNL,* with a series of comedy sketches followed by a musical guest artist. Thelma quickly evolved into the oldest bodyguard in the business and then the "security guard" for *All That.* Often the setup would be that the guest artist would try to pass by Thelma, who always demanded to see a backstage pass, which in the interests of comedy, they never, ever had. This would usually lead to Thelma getting steamed, sputtering and stomping until suddenly the guest artist would produce her favorite food and be let in without delay.

Both Justin and Britney guest-starred on the show during Jamie Lynn's time there, and both were harassed mercilessly by ol' Thelma. In Britney and Jamie Lynn's sketch, Thelma did a riff on Britney's song titles, threatening, among other things, to "hit you, baby, one more time!" Britney was carrying bacon in her purse, naturally, and Thelma ended up accepting pork as her all-access pass.

It was great fun. When she was on *All That*, Jamie Lynn was about the same age Britney had been when she was on *The Mickey Mouse Club*. She absolutely loved every minute of it, and the show was a wonderful training ground, just as *MMC* had been for Britney. When I look back at that time, especially at that sketch with my two girls, I see now that was as good as it gets. My two daughters, healthy and whole, were bouncing their creative energy off one another, working from that essential sister chemistry, where each one made the other shine. And shine they did. As Britney and Jamie Lynn's mom, I couldn't ask for more.

Zoey 101

Jamie Lynn loved acting, then and now, and what better way to make a living than to do what you love? Just as Amanda Bynes had gotten her start on *All That* and eventually ended up with her own series, *The Amanda Show*, the show was a springboard for Jamie Lynn's dream come true too.

Nickelodeon's *Zoey 101* is about a young lady named Zoey Brooks, who is among the first girls to attend a formerly all-boys school. The premise was Jamie Lynn's idea, too, and when she pitched it to Dan Schneider, again, he went for it. Viewers seem to enjoy *Zoey* as well: in 2006, Jamie Lynn won the award for Favorite TV Actress at the 2006 Kids' Choice Awards. Of course, it's not about awards or red carpets or any of that. It's the satisfaction of doing well what you love to do, and being yourself while you do it! I have always told Jamie Lynn to just be herself, and everything will fall into place.

My youngest child has definitely taken a different road than her big brother or sister. She can actually sing beautifully, too, but she has always wanted something different for herself. The theme song of *Zoey 101*, called "Follow Me," is cowritten by Britney and sung by Jamie Lynn.

> I NEVER HAD A MOMENT'S ANXIETY ABOUT HER PARTYING OR DRINKING OR SMOKING, THE THINGS I WRUNG MY HANDS OVER WITH HER SIBLINGS. ALWAYS CONSCIENTIOUS, JAMIE LYNN RARELY, IF EVER, EVEN MISSED CURFEW.

Honestly, I didn't worry too much about my baby girl, my old soul. She has always been reserved and slow to anger, which should be almost a genetic impossibility, coming from her family! I never had a moment's anxiety about her partying or drinking or smoking, the things I wrung my hands over with her siblings. Always conscientious, Jamie Lynn rarely, if ever, even missed curfew.

She has also seen, if not firsthand a close secondhand, the pitfalls around every corner when you have the level of fame Britney has. That's not something Jamie Lynn ever wanted for herself.

She's close to the Lord, and to her family and friends, and she's rooted in our community, which has always been grounding for her, come what may. In some ways, Jamie Lynn was the ideal teenager, but as I was to discover in the not-too-distant future, even my ideal teenager was only human.

Why Did I Say Yes—Again?

People always want to know, why did I let my younger daughter get into show business if I could see what effect fame had on my older daughter? When people ask me that, I think they are assuming that I was already well acquainted with the negative side of life in the public eye—the bad press, the paparazzi hunting us all down like animals, the utter lack of privacy, and so on. At that time, it was pretty much all good. In fact, it was fantastic in some ways. When Jamie Lynn turned thirteen, for example, Columbia Pictures flew her and thirteen of her best friends—plus me and my friends as chaperones—to an exclusive screening of *13 Going on 30* with the movie's star, Jennifer Garner, in attendance. Just seven years prior, I was scraping together hot dogs and potato salad for her birthday party!

Here's what people don't realize: it was 2002 then, the year Jamie Lynn started on *All That*, and one of the best years of Britney's career. She was voted the most powerful celebrity by *Forbes* magazine on their list of the top one hundred most powerful people in Hollywood. Not that it was ever about "power," but for Britney to top that list signified that things were going extremely well in her career—and her life. She was still in a loving, committed relationship (until March of that year), and she just *looked* happy.

The thing I always look at in my children is their demeanor. Most every mother has an awareness of what's truly going on in her child's heart and soul. It's like a really strong perception, a channel from the mother's spirit to the child's. One look at Britney's face told me everything I needed to know. She could always put you at ease with her warmth and with a smile that could light up a cold, dark room in the dead of winter. The world was smiling with her, embracing her sweet, endearing temperament. That was such a good time for her. She was only looking forward to good things to come.

So, why did I say yes—again—to my second daughter, allowing her to pursue her own dreams? Because back then, there was no bad side— or if there was, it was far outweighed by the good elements. If only I had known that within a few years, the bad would far outweigh the good.

twenty-one

BRITNEY AND KEVIN

&

On the face of things, Britney's troubles started around the time she gave birth to her beloved surprise baby, Jayden, but I could see that she was having problems much sooner than that.

My mother's radar definitely went up after the phone call I received from her on January 3, 2004, when she told me she had married Jason Alexander, a kid from home, in Las Vegas. At first, I thought she was telling me a distinctly unfunny joke, but when I realized she really had married him, I was not pleased, to put it mildly. "What were you thinking?" I chastised. "That's the stupidest thing I have ever heard of!"

Oddly enough, my first thought, besides being ticked off, was a memory of little Jason, being chased around my day care with a broom by my sister, Sandra. He was a pretty naughty tyke, and I will never forget my even-keeled sister calling me from work, telling me she had had to chase that boy all over the place and finally treed him up on top of the Coke machine! "What am I supposed to do with him?" she asked, exasperated. I can't even remember what I said, but I do remember her next remark: "Now, Lynne, it would be the worst curse in the world if one of our girls grew up to marry this one." Darn it all if one of mine didn't go and do just that.

Fuming, I called Jamie and Bryan, and then I flew out to Nevada myself to get to the bottom of it. By the time I got there, she and Jason had sobered up, in more ways than one. "Is this what you want?" I asked. They both shook their heads. No, of course this wasn't what they wanted, but it happened anyway. They had the marriage annulled quickly, and the whole thing was over before it started.

It was reckless and irresponsible, and out of character for Britney, which clued me in to the fact that something was going on with my daughter. Almost two years after she and Justin had broken up, Britney was still wounded. To add insult to injury, she had been beaten to death in the press over her annulled marriage and because her third album was not performing as well as the first two. She was starting to act out of her pain, and the catch was, she had the money to party and jet-set to her heart's content, all in an effort to numb her disappointment and heartache. Well, actually there was more than one catch: Britney was living in a fishbowl, and every false move she made was duly noted by millions of people all over the world. She could run, but there was no place on earth my child could hide.

> BRITNEY WAS LIVING IN A FISHBOWL, AND EVERY FALSE MOVE SHE MADE WAS DULY NOTED BY MILLIONS OF PEOPLE ALL OVER THE WORLD. SHE COULD RUN, BUT THERE WAS NO PLACE ON EARTH MY CHILD COULD HIDE.

Kevin

Within three months after the Jason Alexander fiasco, Britney had met a young man, Kevin Federline, who had worked as a backup dancer for

Justin, Christina, and other big pop acts. I liked amiable Kevin, because he was down-to-earth and kindhearted. Of course, I wasn't crazy about the fact that he was already a daddy, and that his ex-girlfriend was then eight months pregnant with their second child. What mother would be? I advised Britney to take it slow, but you can sometimes advise your adult child all you want and the message just does not get through. She didn't *want* to take it slow. In fact, their relationship galloped along so quickly they were engaged in a matter of three more months, in July, and by September they were married.

People want to know if I gave my blessing to Britney and Kevin, and the answer is, not really. I wanted them to give their relationship more time; it's that simple. I also didn't want to alienate her by haranguing her constantly about this. She knew full well that I felt things were moving way too fast, and I didn't understand why she and Kevin had to get married in such short order. Why not just date and see what happens? But Britney was drawn to Kevin's stability and his wholehearted acceptance of her. She wanted to feel grounded, and he gave her that feeling of security she had been craving.

There is not a mean bone in Kevin's body, and he really is such a good daddy. I've often thought that if the Lord got hold of Kevin, he could do great things with him. Unfortunately, Britney and Kevin's marriage only lasted a little more than two years, just long enough for Britney to give birth to Preston and Jayden. Preston had been born a year after Britney and Kevin got married, in September 2005. Jayden arrived just a year and two days after Preston.

To have two children so close together would be overwhelming for any woman. I believe Britney had postpartum depression, which, added to her brokenhearted spirit over the end of her marriage to Kevin and the enormous pressures of her career, brought her to the breaking point. So many things in her life hadn't turned out the way she wanted them to.

The media's flogging of Britney intensified after she married Kevin, and the two of them had no peace at all as a couple. And when she became a mother, the scrutiny and judgment escalated to an unendurable point. When she fled the paparazzi, with baby Preston on her lap, for example, the verdict came down hard: *Britney Spears is a bad mother.* Then there was the time she tripped while holding Preston, and a bodyguard caught him just in time. How many mothers have stumbled while holding their babies? How has America become so self-righteous? That's what I really want to know.

Fault Lines

By the time Britney and Kevin split up in November 2006, she was in trouble. When she came home for Christmas with the babies, I could tell she was sad and restless. Plus she was losing her aunt Sandra; we all were, and that added to her pain.

What I didn't know then (did anybody know?) was how much she was truly suffering.

twenty-two

SANDRA LEAVES

It was around Thanksgiving 2006 when I finally got it through my thick skull that there was nothing I could do to hold my sister to this earth—to me, her children, and my children. Sandra was slipping away from us.

There wasn't a shocking test result or some doctor giving us a number of months or weeks she had left. One day, though, I finally saw a fundamental change in Sandra. You could no longer see the joy in her. It had gone, and in its place came resignation. Without her saying one word, I could just sense that she was no longer concentrating on the here and now. Sandra was almost fierce in her determination to get certain things done. Christmas presents that year had to be absolutely perfect and carried out to a tee per her specifications. Her superfocused attitude almost reminded me of a pregnant woman about to give birth, in a frenzy of preparations nesting for the new life to come. Or a busy farm wife who puts up corn and tomatoes against the day when nothing would grow in the dark wintertime. Sandra was making provisions for us against the day when she wouldn't be here anymore. It would be a new life for her in heaven and a different kind of new life for us, without her.

One of the Christmas presents Sandra arranged for during this time was for Bryan, whom she adored. She never called it a preparation period, or even referred to dying at all. But in retrospect, I see that's what she was doing: preparing. You could tell she was trying to finish up a job. My son had become so special and dear to her in the last few years of her life, and she planned the ideal gift for him: a framed photo of the two of them at the beach. This was a lot more complicated than it sounds at first. Bryan is so picky about his photos; he doesn't think he's photogenic at all. So Sandra found a wonderful photo of him that she knew would meet with his approval, had herself digitally added in next to him, and then had a beautiful beach background put in as the setting. She loved the beach so much, especially Britney's condo in Florida. Today, Bryan has this treasured keepsake of his aunt Sandra. Somehow she knew we would need mementoes like that to hold on to in the very near future.

Sandra's Unbroken Circle

For the last few weeks of her life, Sandra was cared for by so many people who meant the most to her. Friends and family rallied with deliveries of food, medicine, cards, and loving visits. Their touches of grace and kindness warmed her waning days on this earth, and I will always be so thankful to them for their gifts of service and love.

But at the very end, when Sandra wanted almost no company, the core circle of love included me; Sandra's husband, Reggie; her daughter, Laura Lynne; Laura Lynne's boyfriend, Blaine; and Sandra's best friend, Kathy. She did not want to have hospice care set up for her or to have strangers tending her at the end. Fortunately, God gave us the wherewithal to meet many of her needs between the five of us, with the support of a visiting nurse and also Sandra's doctor, who came by frequently.

That's just one of the benefits of a small town, the care extended so freely from one person to another when it's needed. The doctor and other medical professionals who came by the house came because they loved us and didn't charge us a bit. In LA, you could get a doctor to make a house call if you forked over hundreds of dollars, but in Kentwood that's just the way things were done—and are done to this day.

I have some precious memories of those last days together, memories that are at once painful and beautiful. It was a blessing to care for Sandra's most mundane needs, such as giving her foot rubs. She was comforted when I would rub her feet as a distraction from the pain; I had learned how to give a good foot rub back when Mama had rheumatoid arthritis so badly. It was something small yet meaningful that I could still do for my big sister, and if you've watched someone you adore die slowly and painfully, you know how meaningful those foot rubs were for me.

One day Kathy had been sleeping in a chair, and I wanted her to be more comfortable, so I suggested she crawl in with Sandra, as I had been doing some nights. We all thought Sandra was sleeping, because she was at a stage in her decline where she was hardly saying much at all. Then all of the sudden, she called out from her bed, in a voice that was anything but feeble: "Kathy, you're not sleepin' in my bed!" For some reason, it made us all laugh a little because it was so unexpected and out of character for gentle Sandra.

She loved Kathy dearly, so I know it wasn't that she was mad at her or anything. The thing is, I was her little sister, and we always used to sleep together when we were at home. I used to fling my leg over her legs and nuzzle my nose into her back, and that's how we slept for years until she left for college. That night, so close to her last one on this earth, Sandra wanted us to be as we were, sisters who shared everything. So of course I crawled into bed with her and treasured every second.

all had the same idea, but we hadn't told one another we were coming. We sat on that grassy hillside, which overlooks a huge dairy farm; each of us silent and then talkative by turns, remembering.

Somehow, Sandra was gone, and the three of us were left behind.

twenty-three

THE BREAKDOWN

Two weeks after Sandra died, I watched in utter dismay and shock as footage of my beautiful daughter shaving off her hair aired on national TV. The look in her eyes as she stared into the camera was desperately forlorn, angry, and belligerent, all at once. I just wept, praying almost incoherently that God would safeguard my daughter from harm. *Just be with her. Just protect her*, I prayed over and over again.

What in the world was going on in her mind?

Clearly, something inside of her had broken and needed to be healed. We—Jamie and I, Larry, and other members of her team—felt she needed to check in somewhere and just chill. She was hurting so badly—that was obvious—and she needed to stop running from the pain and address it. The day before she shaved her head, Britney had stayed less than twenty-four hours at an off-shore drug rehabilitation facility in Antigua, and obviously that had not worked out. We had heard good things about Promises, a rehab center in Malibu, where she could have intensive counseling and receive some blessed solace from the media hounding her night and day. I wanted her to go to Promises, but Britney didn't want to, and she was livid at me for trying to "force" her to. She ended up staying there for a month.

When she was gone, I tried to help out with the boys as much as I could, as I stayed in LA for much of that month. I reminded them often that their mama loved them and would come back to them as soon as she was able.

Kevin, meanwhile, was making all the right choices. He was a calm, caring daddy, firm with their behavior.

> KEVIN, MEANWHILE, WAS MAKING ALL THE RIGHT CHOICES DURING THIS TIME. HE WAS A CALM, CARING DADDY, FIRM WITH THEIR BEHAVIOR.

Later, Britney would lash out at me, accusing me of siding with Kevin and "letting" him have the boys while she was at Promises. But I didn't have nearly as much say as she must have thought I had. Kevin is their father, and he had every legal right to have them. There wasn't much I could do. If it had been up to me, I would have taken Preston and Jayden home with me to Louisiana.

When she is at her best, Britney is an amazing mother. After she had Preston, she was the most protective, attentive parent; I rarely saw that baby off her hip. She was always kissing him and singing to him and could not wipe the smile off her face. I never saw a mama so goo-goo over her baby. In good times, she is so excited and proud to be the boys' mama, and she's full of plans for what kinds of activities they can do when they're together. But during this time period, she wasn't at her best, to say the least.

She got out of rehab after a month, and I could see right away that it hadn't provided the healing Britney needed in her life. All it did was slow her down a little bit, and her anger at me had not cooled. In fact, she refused to speak to me, and our estrangement would last an excruciating seven months.

It was hard for me to believe this much-loved daughter, my very *heart*, was enduring such pain in her life, and I couldn't be there beside her to help her heal. I was in a dark place, discouraged, and wondering how we could have come to this drifting apart, and now this total rift. Everything I had prayed for—her healing, her stability, a true reconciliation between a mother and daughter who had always been kindred spirits—had not come to pass.

I felt hopeless, as though I was losing my grasp on my child, maybe forever.

twenty-four

THE PAPARAZZI

When Britney beat that paparazzo's car with her umbrella, she was acting out my fantasy.

Of all the dark aspects of fame, dealing with the tabloid media, with their shady reporters and rabid photographers, has to be the darkest. And it has gotten so much worse, even in the last five years.

I remember the first time I was really angry at something the press had printed about Britney. She was on her second concert tour, in 2001, and they were criticizing her for having gained a couple of pounds. She picked up the newspaper, read the story, and started crying. My heart sank when I read it; it was so mean-spirited, overblown, and hurtful.

I was still naive enough to be surprised—and infuriated.

That day I started at ground zero with the tabloids, at the beginning of my learning how to endure the media fallout of Britney's fame. I told her bodyguard to keep any kind of negative press away from her. Of course, I can see now that was like protecting your home with one sandbag when a flood was coming. And this was just a drop in the bucket, the first drop of a deluge yet to come.

For some reason, after 2002, the negative attention from the tabloids and the paparazzi escalated. I don't know if it was the fact that Britney and Justin had broken up, that her third album hadn't done as spectacularly well as the first two, or if it was a reflection that our culture had taken a turn for the worst, or all of the above. It seemed to me that all of a sudden, people were much more interested in the negative things, salacious tidbits about famous people's private lives. There used to be more integrity in journalism, even with the tabloids. Where are people's manners, their common decency toward one another?

> THERE USED TO BE MORE INTEGRITY IN JOURNALISM, EVEN WITH THE TABLOIDS. WHERE ARE PEOPLE'S MANNERS, THEIR COMMON DECENCY TOWARD ONE ANOTHER?

In the past, a reporter would identify herself as such and ask if she could talk to me. Now, I can be standing in line at Starbucks, at the grocery store, or the dry cleaners, and strike up a friendly conversation with a pleasant stranger, only to find out a few days later that I have given an "exclusive" to a tabloid magazine. It makes it very hard to know whom to trust. In fact, the last "pleasant stranger" a tabloid sent wasn't pleasant at all; he creeped me out. This so-called magazine stooped as low as to plant someone on an airplane in the hopes that he could get me to divulge some deep, dark secret about my family. It was pretty awful, when I realized later what had happened. I mean, you just wouldn't believe this guy . . . what a piece of work! Because it still makes me mad, I'm going to tell you about the whole sordid deal, because, by golly, I want all of you to shake your heads and join me in a big collective *Tsk-tsk. What is this world coming to?*

The Guy on the Plane

I was coming from LA in April 2008, after spending some time with Britney and the boys. From the very beginning, we have had a great relationship with Delta Airlines. One of their reps is always so kind to me, and he often arranges for me to have a seat in the bulkhead section, with a seat open next to me. I always have a book to read, and this time was no exception.

I smiled at the nice man next to me, and I settled in with a pillow against the window and opened my book. Lost in the story, I barely noticed what was going on two seats down from me, although I was vaguely aware that the man was getting up from his seat, which was strange because the plane was all set to take off. I glanced over and saw that he was flustered, sighing and struggling to get his stuff out of the overhead compartment. Then another man took his place, a short guy in his early thirties, wearing strange cowboy clothes and flashing an overly eager look on his face. My radar immediately picked up on something strange.

"Whatcha reading?" he asked, peering at my book.

"Murder mystery," I said shortly, immediately turning back to my book.

"Is it good?" he asked.

"Yes. As a matter of fact, I can't put this down." I was hoping he would take the hint, because 99 percent of the population would catch a clue that I didn't want to have a heart-to-heart conversation right then!

I napped for about an hour and a half, and when I returned to my seat after a visit to the bathroom, he revved up his questions again. His *loud* questions.

"Where are you from?"

"New Orleans," I evaded. *Does he know somehow whose mother I am?*

"Do you like it there?"

"Yes, it's my home."

"Do you have any kids?"

"Yes."

"Boys or girls?"

"A boy and two girls."

"Boy! You read fast. You went from chapter 28 to chapter 40!" he belted out.

My discomfort grew. Who watches you closely enough to know which chapters you started and ended at? I tried to turn away and keep reading, but he kept talking and talking, and my inborn Southern politeness just would not let me rudely ignore him. I know, I should've just shut him down like a bad Broadway musical, but that's just not the way I'm wired. But I'm working on it!

He began to tell me a sob story about how he had been struggling to make it in Hollywood, and how the people there are *such* sharks. I nodded politely, not smiling or encouraging him in any way, shape, or form. When that didn't get a rise out of me, he started telling me he was a person of faith, and how his church had helped him overcome so much in his life. The problem is, none of it rang true. My first thought was that he wanted me to help him get his foot in the door in show business. *He's baiting me*, I thought. *He wants me to break down and tell him who I am so he can ask me for help with getting some connections.*

"As long as a person stays with God, he'll be okay," the man said.

"Yes," I agreed, and turned to the window.

Well, that wasn't even the end of it. We were on our descent when I was appalled to realize that this man had stood up and was leaning over the space between us—and me—and looking out my window.

"Is that the Mississippi?" he bellowed. I'm sure people could hear him several rows back. "It sure is big!"

I was cringing, totally disbelieving that this yokel was so blatantly invading my personal space! "Cowboy Cal" must have stood that way for three or four minutes, when the flight attendant finally told him to sit down.

I'm sure you could hear him five rows down!

When the flight ended, he just said good-bye and left. He couldn't even say, "Nice to meet you," because we hadn't really ever met, nor had we exchanged even our names. That's what makes what happened later so shocking, but I'm getting ahead of myself . . . A couple of people from the flight told me how sorry they were this man had been so obnoxious. "We knew who you were, but never would have said anything. We couldn't believe the nerve of that guy!" When Kathy picked me up, we went out for oyster po' boys, and I told her about this odd man on the airplane. We kind of laughed about it, and I forgot all about him.

A couple of days later, I got a call from Jamie Lynn's business manager. "Did you give an exclusive to *Life and Style* magazine?" she asked, incredulous. "No!" I said, scrambling to think of who I had talked to recently—which nice little old lady at the grocery store or sweet twenty-something manicurist could have tricked me into giving an "interview"? This had happened before, and those kinds of experiences served to make me even more guarded with strangers.

Lou called the magazine and demanded to know what had happened. They admitted they had "planted" a reporter on the airplane and said that he had given me his card and told me up front he was from this magazine. He most assuredly had done neither. Nor did I say one word to him about my daughter, other than to admit I *had* two daughters. When he couldn't get anything out of me, this man, unashamedly and manifestly, fabricated the whole shootin' match!

Here's a snippet of my "exclusive interview":

On April 20, Lynne finally broke her silence, giving an exclusive, emotional interview. . . . And she didn't hold back . . .

When asked about Jamie Lynn, now 17, Lynne spoke frankly. "I'm a bit disappointed that my youngest daughter got pregnant at such an early age. All I can do is turn to God for answers and just leave it in his hands."

But despite her frustration over the situation Jamie Lynn has gotten herself into, Lynne is trying to look on the bright side. "Jamie Lynn will be a wonderful mother," she says. "She really has a way with children—she's a natural nurturer. I just wish she had waited a bit."

Later, the magazine stood behind their reporter, who had told them, apparently, that he had given me his card and identified himself as a reporter from their offices.

It's hard for me to believe some in the profession of journalism have stooped so low as to *plant* people on planes. It really is all about the mighty buck these days, isn't it?

The interesting thing is who they sent. If the magazine had assigned a congenial young woman, or a motherly older lady to try and interview me, I may have said just those kinds of things to her, had she told me honestly who she was and what she wanted. But I never would have opened up one little bit to a smarmy, opportunistic person like that fellow!

I'm not saying every magazine has treated us this way. *People*, in particular, has been fair to us. But certain tabloid magazines have sunk lower and lower in their quest to get their hands on some dirt. Often, they interview some "source" who has an ax to grind with our family for some reason.

> I'M NOT SAYING EVERY MAGAZINE HAS TREATED US THIS WAY. *PEOPLE*, IN PARTICULAR, HAS BEEN FAIR TO US. BUT CERTAIN TABLOID MAGAZINES HAVE SUNK LOWER AND LOWER IN THEIR QUEST TO GET THEIR HANDS ON SOME DIRT.

The Quest for Dirt

People still think they can believe everything they read. If that were true, then I would be a money-hungry, neglectful, pushy "stage mom" (why doesn't anyone ever get called a "stage dad"?). When I read something like that, especially something that's not only untrue but patently vicious, I go through a gamut of emotions. It's a mixture of anger, hurt, and bewilderment—how can they say these things? Over the years, I have developed a thicker skin when it comes to the mudslinging. A certain callousness develops, probably a protective mechanism. It's usually best to just ignore it and go about my business, and that's what I most often do.

But when something is printed about our family that is really below the belt, I admit it does hurt. It's then that I get on my knees and pray. *God, you know who I am. You know what I've done and haven't done. You know the real me. Please remind me of who I am and who you created me to be.*

When I need some human reassurance, I pick up the phone and call someone from home, a friend who knows everything about me, who can instantly sort out a lie from the truth. Sometimes I just need a friend to talk me through it, and then I feel much better.

At times, people have asked me why I don't just sue whatever magazine or TV show is spreading lies about my family. It's almost assumed that if I don't bring a lawsuit against someone, then whatever he or she said must be true. Have you ever noticed how few celebrities sue the tabloids? That's because it just doesn't pay. You can spend hundreds of thousands of dollars and months and months of time and energy, and your only payoff will be a tiny retraction, in the smallest font known to fonts, buried in the back pages of the magazine.

As a rule, it's simply not worth it.

A *Thousand Words*

A picture is worth a thousand words, and sometimes, it can be worth millions of dollars too. Even if people discount what is printed in a magazine, it's hard to argue with a photo. But don't be deceived; photos can be distorted in any number of ways.

I'm not talking about airbrushing here; we all know when a woman past forty has no wrinkles, something is going on. I'm talking about the ways that some photographers get the photos in the first place, and then what they do with those photos to tell their own version of the story.

For example, the magazines often use photos of my grandsons crying on their covers. First of all, why in this free country of ours has "free speech" turned into "anything goes"? Why isn't it necessary to obtain permission from a child's parents to have a photo of that child published in a magazine, never mind the cover? We are used to seeing the adorable faces of celebrity babies on the covers of magazines, to see Suri Cruise and Violet Affleck and Preston and Jayden splashed all over the newsstand, but do we ever stop to wonder how those photos were obtained?

It truly puzzles me why it's even legal for magazines to use a photo of my grandsons without first asking for clearance from Kevin or Britney.

> JAYDEN AND PRESTON ARE GENERALLY HAPPY BOYS, SMILING AND CONTENT, BUT BY THEIR USE OF THOSE CRYING PHOTOS, THE MAGAZINES CAN PAINT A PICTURE OF TWO MISERABLE CHILDREN.

And then there are the crying photos. The reason those boys are crying is they are scared of all those flashbulbs going off in their faces, all those men shouting, and the chaos and noise. What toddler wouldn't be scared of that kind of commotion? In their everyday lives, Jayden and Preston are generally happy boys, smiling and content, but by their use of those crying photos, the magazines can paint a picture of two miserable children. I cannot for the life of me look at those magazine covers, because it kills me. That's when I want to bring out my umbrella and beat someone!

You wouldn't believe the methods the rag media use to get information and photos. Digging through garbage? That's the least of it. You can go ahead and dive right into my Dumpster and rummage around my crumpled receipts and bills and pizza boxes, but don't endanger someone by chasing me and my family at one hundred miles per hour. I agree with George Clooney, who recently spoke out against the "bounty hunter" frame of mind that's become the norm for most paparazzi. He is referring to the practice of the paparazzi culture, which sets a price on a certain photo—say, a movie star's first "baby bump" or a picture that "proves" that a certain star is dating another star. When the price is high, those photographers will stop at nothing to capture that big money shot. I recently found out that the "bounty" on the first photo of Jamie Lynn's baby bump was a hundred thousand dollars, with the probably added bonus of another three hundred thousand for worldwide rights. Is it just me, or is that just plain disturbing? These members of the "media" will push and shove each other, run red lights, engage in high-speed chases, and drive extremely close to the car being driven by the celebrity—it can degenerate quickly into a very dangerous situation.

Clooney even took up for Britney, defending her somewhat for running that red light. "There's eight guys with cameras at night in the middle of the street," he told *Entertainment Tonight*, referring to the video footage. "There are no rules now. It's getting to the point where people who are not involved are getting hurt."

Thankfully, most of the time the paparazzi are simply a nuisance, but you never know when a harassing situation will turn into a hazardous one. They even endanger themselves! A few years ago, I was with Britney, Jamie Lynn, and Crystal in a parking lot of a pet store on Wilshire Boulevard, trying to put my car in reverse. But I couldn't, because there was a photographer clinging to my car, insisting he get a shot. I waited and waited for him to get the clue that I wasn't going to give him anything, but he was insistent. Finally, I nudged the car in reverse, just a couple of inches, to give him a strong hint that I intended to leave. That blooming idiot was hanging on my back window! I began to back out very slowly, thinking surely he would jump off. And then I accidentally ran over his foot. Well, I really *didn't* run over his foot—or I would have felt it—but he accused me of doing just that and called the police.

I was delighted to tell my version of events to the kind officer, who laughed when I suggested they follow the man to the hospital. "He's liable to smash his foot with a sledgehammer and sue *me* for it!" I said. Naturally, we never heard another thing about it, so obviously his foot healed fast.

Britney has it ten times worse than me. It's a wonder that girl hasn't run over dozens of paparazzi feet in her day!

I've often thought it was strange that the tabloid media appears to break all kinds of laws, and then throw their hands up in the air and say, "Hey, I'm doing my job." Clooney's motorcycle wreck wasn't the only accident caused by paparazzi, not by a long shot. There have been several wrecks that have happened because they were chasing Britney, and sometimes Preston and Jayden. In Louisiana, it's illegal to endanger the lives of innocent people while in pursuit of a photo, just as it won't fly to park for days on end on private property. Members of the tabloid media who have tried that at my house have been escorted out of town by the police.

Interestingly, what's legal, and what's not, changes somewhat in Los Angeles, or at least it seems to. There, in my experience, almost anything goes when it comes to the paparazzi and the way they prey on celebrities. The law appears to turn a blind eye to high-speed chases and invasion of privacy. *Oh, but that's what you get when you're famous*, the conventional wisdom seems to be. *You knew this was part of the deal when you signed on to become a star.*

The truth is, we didn't. No one could have envisioned, even five or six years ago, the way the tabloid media would ramp up their coverage, to the point where a star is eventually forced to release photos of his or her newborn baby *somewhere*; otherwise, that celebrity's family members may be in danger from aggressive photographers. I can't speak for Tom Cruise or Ben Affleck or Julia Roberts, but I do know my family did not have the faintest idea that someday our daughters would not be able to walk around freely in their own backyards without someone jumping out of the bushes to take their picture. I don't care how famous you are, that's an invasion of privacy. Fame does have a price, and part of that price is sacrificing your privacy—to an extent. But where are the lines, and what are the consequences if they are crossed?

> She has seventeen full-time paparazzi assigned to her, night and day, which means they are her constant shadow, at Starbucks, at the grocery store, at a restaurant. Britney literally cannot escape them.

Britney has been accused of encouraging the media, of "courting" them in a way. I'm not going to speak for her one way or another, but one observation I have had is that she may not be courting them so much as just coping with them. If you have an incurable, chronic disease, you learn to live with the symptoms the best way you can. She has seventeen full-time paparazzi assigned to her, night and day, which means they are her constant shadow, at Starbucks, at the grocery store, at a restaurant. Britney literally cannot escape them. They are in her life for the duration, so why not make the best of it? As far as I can tell, she has no choice.

Under a Microscope

Never would I have imagined how my daughters, and to a certain extent the whole family, would come to live under a microscope. And how the multitudes would become our judge and jurors to proclaim to the whole world who and what kind of people we are. If I were to defend my family from every untruth and half-truth and twisted truth that has been printed or broadcast, this book would have to be expanded to a ten-volume set!

People think they know us from all the stories they've read, and so they feel it's quite all right to pass judgment. Sometimes the public's verdict, no matter how misguided, hurts. But I am learning to deflect that hurt, more and more. One thing I have learned, though, especially lately, is that it is a superficial judgment at best, a shallow opinion that just barely scratches the surface of the truth. Those who really know us know our hearts and what kind of people we truly are. My faith teaches me that God's opinion matters most, and that's what I hold on to, no matter what is printed or said.

Britney and I saying goodbye
on her way to Sweden.

Britney and I on top of the world.

Laura Lynne, Jessica, Britney, Jamie Lynn, Caitlin, and me on a blissful vacation to the Caribbean. Sandra was back at the condo, feeling sick. The trip was Britney's Christmas gift to her.

Jamie Lynn and I on vacation in Destin, Florida.

Precious moments with my first grandchild, Sean Preston
Federline

Preston and his mama at his first birthday party.

Protective big brother Bryan and Jamie Lynn.

My inseparable other half, Sandra, and her daughter, my "third" daughter, Laura Lynne.

Beau is so small he jumps in my purse when he knows I'm leaving.

twenty-five

MY GRANDBABIES

The first time I had both grandsons in my arms was one night soon after Jayden was born. I offered to babysit, because I knew Britney and Kevin needed time together, and besides, I was dying to have those little ones all to myself! I had fourteen-month-old Preston and two-month-old Jayden in my bed with me as I watched TV. They were both wearing the coziest terry-cloth footie pajamas, and they were both nestled close by my side. It was the warmest, snuggest feeling. It had been a long time since I had babies all cuddled up with me in bed, and I was in grandma heaven.

When you are older and can look back with the wisdom hindsight brings, you see the times that you were on autopilot when you were young. I don't know about you, but I feel as if I didn't really savor the precious moments I had when my own babies were little. I was trying so hard to make a living, to keep them bathed, in clean clothes, with hair combed and nails clipped—essentially, to keep my head and theirs above water. I strove to keep the house tidy and good meals on the table, while juggling their school, extracurricular activities, and keeping up with other family and friends. Basically, I was like every other mother—short on time and with a long laundry list of items to check off before I was satisfied my brood was being raised properly and my house was being managed as it should be.

I wish now I had soaked in the beauty of the moment, taking the time to really enjoy my children when I had them with me. And the truth of the matter is, even when the dishes were done and the homework supervised, I still didn't always savor the little things, because my mind was a thousand miles away—on my marriage, our business troubles, how I would manage to pay the electric company. I don't think I am the only fifty-something mom, however, to look back and think that sometimes she cheated her children out of her undivided attention when they were young. And we all know the person we really cheated was ourselves, because we can't get those years back.

Me Maw, Paw Paw and the boys having fun in the sun.

Sometimes when you become a grandparent, you can redeem some of that lost time and pour it into your grandchildren. I look at Preston (who is Britney Jean, all over again) and Jayden, and I am determined to delight in them with my whole heart and mind, giving them all the energy and focus and excitement I have and they deserve. Mothers, all we can really do is learn from our mistakes, golden time misspent, and do better in the here and now. Right now, I want to play, nurture, and be present with my grandchildren in every valuable moment I am given.

Preston

Britney had been trying to get pregnant. I thought she should hold off on that a bit, seeing as she and Kevin had only been married for a few months. A marriage needs time to "settle," I told her, and there was plenty of time for children later on. But I couldn't help feeling a little bit excited, too, at the prospect of a grandbaby, which is why my girlfriend and I drove to the drugstore one day and bought Britney a pregnancy test. Can you imagine the flurry of media attention Britney would have had if she had been the one to pick up that test? The paparazzi would have flocked to Kentwood sooner than you could say, "Stork."

> I DROVE TO THE DRUGSTORE ONE DAY AND BOUGHT BRITNEY A PREGNANCY TEST. CAN YOU IMAGINE THE FLURRY OF MEDIA ATTENTION BRITNEY WOULD HAVE HAD IF SHE HAD BEEN THE ONE TO PICK UP THAT TEST? THE PAPARAZZI WOULD HAVE FLOCKED TO KENTWOOD SOONER THAN YOU COULD SAY, "STORK."

Britney and Kevin were visiting us in Louisiana, and she took the test at home. She broke the news to Kevin first, and then to her family: they were expecting! I was over the moon. At the time, I wasn't even fifty yet, although my age was the last thing on my mind. All I could think of was that there was a beloved little one coming to us, a sweet baby to read storybooks to and bake cookies with and rock to sleep. And when I found out the baby was a boy, I couldn't wait. Instantly, memories of baby Bryan flooded my mind, and I was sure this baby would be every bit as sweet and gorgeous as my own boy. Of course, I was right. Sean Preston Federline stole my heart from the moment I saw him.

Roots

I wish I could tell you that I had a wonderful, tight bond with my own grandparents and that those memories informed the way I relate to my own grandbabies. But it wouldn't be true.

My mother's parents were British, and I never even met my maternal grandfather. My Grandmother Portell was a classic English bulldog type of lady—bossy, and with starch to spare.

I knew Daddy's parents better, but not much, even though we would visit them every Sunday after dinner. They were aged and sickly by the time I was old enough to remember them.

Britney was crazy about her great-grandma Lexie, and the feeling went both ways. I have a clear memory of this dear lady, running up and down the hill by our house with her thrilled great-granddaughter in a wagon. That was one tough old bird! Folks in town knew her from the fish shop where she worked, and let me tell you, she had a reputation for being a touch crusty. But her soft spots were Jamie and our kids. We couldn't have done without her, literally; when I ran my day care, I'd breast-feed baby Britney early in the morning and turn her over to Grandma Lexie's care while I went to work. She was such a godsend.

What *does* shape my impressions of grandparenthood are my memories of how my parents and Jamie's, and his Grandma Lexie loved on my kids. When Bryan was little, he spent many hours with Mama when I was trying to finish my degree. She absolutely adored him, and he returned her affection in full measure. Sometimes he would spend the night with my mother at the dairy farm where I grew up. They would get up in the morning, and she would give him delicious pastries and an itty-bitty demitasse cup filled with hot chocolate. Mama would take him to the barn, and as she would feed the calves, Bryan would hold the milk buckets. My boy was just learning to talk, and he picked up on his grandma's English accent and would say words like *potato* and *barn* with a crisp British intonation.

By the time Jamie Lynn was born, Mama was already in very bad shape with her arthritis hurting so much, and she died right before Jamie Lynn turned two. I wish both of my parents could have lived to a ripe old age and could have been a real presence in my children's lives, a rock-solid core relationship for them to find shelter and wisdom. Sometimes, I wonder what Mama and Daddy would have said about all of this craziness surrounding Britney, Jamie Lynn, and all of us. They were from another era, a time when character counted more than celebrity, and when your word was your sacred trust. I think the "land of pretend" that is Hollywood would have struck them as another planet in the galaxy altogether, glittery on the surface but spiritually bankrupt underneath. They would have wanted their grandchildren as far away from all that as possible.

I want to be that sturdy, unwavering presence in my own grandchildren's lives, a soft landing place for Preston and Jayden, anchored by the foundation their great-grandparents gave me.

> I WONDER WHAT MAMA AND DADDY WOULD HAVE SAID ABOUT ALL OF THIS CRAZINESS SURROUNDING BRITNEY, JAMIE LYNN, AND ALL OF US. THEY WERE FROM ANOTHER ERA, A TIME WHEN CHARACTER COUNTED MORE THAN CELEBRITY, AND WHEN YOUR WORD WAS YOUR SACRED TRUST.

Me Maw

The boys call me Me Maw, and Jamie, Paw Paw. I know, those titles seem corny and unsophisticated and as old as the hills. I couldn't care less. Whenever one of our grandchildren calls me that, I feel like a queen.

Preston is the more sensitive of the two. He is a tenderhearted little boy who seems more affected by the chaos and the uncertainty in his life. He seems to get sick a bit more than Jayden, who has a horse's constitution. He loves cars, just like my daddy did.

Jayden, who was born one year and two days after his big brother, on September 14, 2006, is both a sweetie and a toughie. Jayden is a happy little guy. Somehow, he seems to have a built-in toughness to combat all the comings and goings and flashbulbs and strange people yelling his name. From day one, this has been his lot in life. Jayden does not know anything different!

Britney and Kevin didn't plan Jayden, and he was a surprise to us all. When she found out she was pregnant, I had a piece of advice from my own experience for her. "Surprise babies are the ones you know are supposed to be here," I said. "They are the Lord's plan and not ours." God knew Preston would need a constant companion and a built-in best friend, someone who would completely understand how it could be strange and normal all at once to live in their unique circumstances. Even if they can't leave the house because people are trying to take their picture, those boys will always have each other.

When I am with them, we play at their sand and water table for hours. We go for walks, play with trucks, and climb on the playground equipment. We roll around on the ground and wrestle, with me blowing raspberries on their little tummies, and them squealing in delight. Usually, the three of us end up in a heap of giggles.

Those boys are my heart.

Angels

On September 12, 2007, amid balloons and party decorations, Kevin, Jamie and I, Preston and Jayden, and some other family members held hands in a circle while a special man named Lonnie blessed our birthday meal of jambalaya and shrimp fettuccine, cooked by Chef Paw Paw. It was the boys' first and second birthday party, a joint event meant to celebrate both of their milestones.

Lonnie is a deacon who teaches regularly at his church. Often, he can be found sitting at a table with his Bible and his commentaries and his notebooks spread out, studying God's Word. He's a huge guy with keen instincts and the heart of a protector, and for all of the above reasons, I am so grateful his job is to be Preston and Jayden's bodyguard.

Lonnie is very intimidating in both his looks and his bearing, and I have no doubt whatsoever that he would lay down his life to protect my grandsons. He loves those boys with all his heart.

That man is an angel, another gift from God to this grandmother, who worries about her little ones and the dangers they face in their surreal world. Lonnie's presence in their home feels, to me, like a conduit of God's protection and security over them.

Another grace channel is Lourdes, Britney's maid for the last two years. That wonderful woman loves the Lord, and she is there for Britney and the boys when I cannot be. They all adore her, as do I.

Their Paw Paw and Me

Jamie went into rehab in 2004 and has been sober for four years. I am proud of his sobriety and happy for all of us that he is no longer drinking.

Today he is walking with the Lord and in some ways is a different, renewed man.

We have been through so much together, both before and after our divorce. During the turbulence of the last couple of years, sometimes it seemed as if he was the one friendly fish swimming with me in a sea of predators. When one of our children is going through something, we are on the phone constantly or else in person, talking things through. In the midst of Britney's difficult summer of 2007, when she and I were at the peak of our estrangement, Jamie and I spent a lot of time together, hashing over our problems with her, grasping at possible solutions, and sometimes just sitting quietly and thinking. In some ways, we are on the same plane more than anyone else; after all, we both love that girl and her siblings more than anyone else in the world.

Of course, we still fight like a married couple sometimes too. We know just how to push each other's buttons, which is why I think we probably won't get remarried—to each other. People ask me if our kids would be happy if we did, and the answer is no. Years ago, after we split up, Britney told a magazine that our divorce was the "best thing that ever happened to our family." She lived through the palpable tension and the screaming matches throughout her growing-up years. So did Bryan and Jamie Lynn, until she was eight years old. No one wants to see a repeat of that.

But then, on the other hand, we have changed as people. With wrinkles and gray hair (Jamie's, not mine!) have come extra grace and maturity and a willingness to be there for each other in a way we never were when we were married.

I will always care about him, just as he will always care about me.

What really gets to me about Jamie is how smitten he is with those grandbabies of ours. It softens my heart toward him whenever I see him with Preston and Jayden. When it comes to them, he is a great big marshmallow! I think it may come as a surprise to the boys when they realize someday that Me Maw and Paw Paw are actually divorced; we spend so much time with them in cograndparenting mode. When we are all in LA, it is quite common for Jamie and me to visit the boys at Britney's house. I'll be in the pool with Preston and Jayden, and Jamie will be grilling something, and then we might all go for a walk. We are much better cograndparents than we ever were as coparents.

The Boys' Reality

One time, Jamie and I were going to take the boys on an outing to see a dinosaur exhibit not far from where they live with their daddy. This was something we had all looked forward to, and I couldn't wait to see the looks on their faces when they saw those dinosaurs. But when the day of the outing came, and we went to pick up the boys at Kevin's house, we couldn't go. There were paparazzi everywhere, swarming like an infestation of bugs. I told a friend of mine that the outing had not gone off as planned. "The paparazzi were too bad," I said. She looked at me, dumbfounded. "Lynne, you make it sound as if the mosquitoes were too thick and you couldn't go to the lake or something." That's exactly how I felt about it too.

It breaks my heart that Preston and Jayden will probably have many occasions to be disappointed because they can't be like other boys and move freely in their world. At least not for the foreseeable future, they won't. But this is the life they were born into. Strange, isn't it, how all the money in the world does not make up

> IT BREAKS MY HEART THAT PRESTON AND JAYDEN WILL PROBABLY HAVE MANY OCCASIONS TO BE DISAPPOINTED BECAUSE THEY CAN'T BE LIKE OTHER BOYS AND MOVE FREELY IN THEIR WORLD.

for the fact that they can't take a walk with their Me Maw and Paw Paw without being photographed, and sometimes they can't leave the house at all?

I wish I could protect them from the cruel world, but Preston and Jayden will have to learn to adjust to their very unique way of life. I want to tell them, *Baby, this is your reality. There are so many people looking at you, and it may seem so strange sometimes. But because people are always going to watch you so closely, you have the chance to do a lot of good in this life.*

I believe kids take their cues from the adults who love them. When you accept as true that things are going to be okay, no matter what, that attitude is conveyed from your spirit to theirs. That's what I have faith in, anyway. I want to teach Preston and Jayden through my encouraging smile and hopeful attitude that they will be okay. Most of all, I want them to know that no matter the circumstances, I would swim through shark-infested waters—literally and figuratively—to get to them. But if for some reason I can't be with them, God is always, *always* by their sides. I hope someday they believe and live from that truth.

twenty-six

"MAMA, I'M PREGNANT"

On December 3, 2007, another windstorm blew through my family, a gust I didn't see coming and one that would flatten us all for a time. What I didn't know then was this: after we had hunkered down and weathered this gale, the green shoots of new life would pop through the ground and bless us anyway. But those blessings were mighty difficult to see on that heartrending day.

For some time, Jamie Lynn had been dating a very nice boy from nearby Mississippi named Casey Aldridge, a young man from a good Christian family, a hardworking, God-fearing family who valued the same things I did. The two of them had met in youth group when Jamie Lynn was about fifteen, and he was a little less than two years older. Casey was (and is) a sweet, well-mannered young man, the kind who would get heavy stuff out of the truck for me and carry in my groceries. Casey was the type of kid who would never even put his shoes on the coffee table—he was everything to like and nothing to worry about.

When Jamie Lynn and I would be in LA for several months out of the year filming *Zoey 101*, Casey would come and visit us, sleeping in the guest room and *not*, as was widely reported, with Jamie Lynn. I liked him, and I liked their relationship, which was very supportive and considerate. But a mother has eyes, and I could see that they were becoming very close, spending every spare moment together. Too close? I didn't think so, but just to be on the safe side, I talked to my daughter once again about matters of sexuality, abstinence, and responsibility to God and yourself. Of course, we'd had these kinds of talks before, but I felt reinforcement wouldn't hurt.

> JAMIE LYNN HAD NEVER DONE A SOLITARY THING TO RAISE EVEN AN EYEBROW, AND SHE CERTAINLY HAD LEFT NOT ONE MINISCULE CLUE AS TO WHAT THEY WERE OBVIOUSLY DOING.

I also had a chat with Casey, issuing some "fatherly threats" and telling him he'd better stay in control around my daughter. He promised me he would and said he would never "hurt her like that."

Was I right in trusting the two of them—two basically good teenagers—taking their word that the relationship was as pure as I hoped and as blameless as I had been led to believe it was? Perhaps I should have questioned them more deeply, but I am telling you, Jamie Lynn had never done a solitary thing to raise even an eyebrow, and she certainly had left not one miniscule clue as to what they were obviously doing. She had always been responsible, and I chose to trust her.

"Tell Me You're Making This Up"

Back to December 3. I was driving up my driveway, returning from a doctor's appointment, when I noticed Casey's truck parked outside. I was surprised, because he wasn't supposed to be there. My firm rule was that the two of them could only see each other on weekends.

Jamie Lynn greeted me at the door and quickly told me Casey had dropped by to pick something up. Then she handed me a folded note and asked me to read it in my room. When I unfolded the note, I read the words that would change all our lives forever: "Mama, I'm pregnant. I am going to keep the baby, and everything is going to be okay."

I thought this was a strange joke at first, a teenager's attempt to yank her mother's chain. But that was wishful thinking, mixed with a healthy knee-jerk dose of denial. Numb, I walked into the living room and looked into my baby girl's unreadable face. Then I glanced hopefully at Casey, and in a heartbreaking second, with one look at his grim face, I knew the contents of the note were true. Instead of the smile I was hoping for, the expression on his face was deathly serious, and he was a nervous wreck, fidgeting and restless. I noticed something else: Casey had his big work boots on my coffee table. That was the last straw.

I felt as if someone punched me in the stomach. My heart was hammering as my brain scrambled to function. I started to pace and rant.

"What about all of our talks?" I cried to Jamie Lynn. "You told me you were a virgin!"

"Mama, would you calm down?" Jamie Lynn said, nervously. But I wasn't going to calm down for a *long* time.

"And you!" I railed at Casey. "You told me you would never hurt her like this!" He didn't say a word. He just hung his head.

They told me that they had already told Casey's parents the news a week beforehand. "We knew how hurt you were going to be," Jamie Lynn said. Hurt? Yes, deeply. I grieved my daughter's innocence and the hard road ahead of her. I was shocked, angry, sad . . . and I also felt foolish for believing them when they told me nothing was going on. *I must be the most naive mother in the world,* I thought.

Later, I called Bryan, Jamie Lynn's big brother, who had always protected her and loved her so much. When I told him his baby sister was pregnant, I could hear over the phone that his heart was ripping out.

"Please, Mama, tell me this is not true!" He was very emotional. That phone call was so hard for me. Almost as hard as my next call, to Jamie Lynn's daddy. Jamie's response was almost identical to Bryan's. His baby was going to have a baby, and it just killed him. "No, no, no, please tell me you're making this up," he pleaded, crying his heart out.

And then there was Britney. How would we tell her this earth-shattering news? I wanted to tell her—we all did—but at the time she had people surrounding her whom we did not trust for one second. We knew if she found out, so would the murky characters running her life at the time. The news would be public as fast as those characters could get to a phone and call the tabloids, and we weren't ready for that—not by a long shot.

I called my best friend, Jill, and took fifteen minutes trying to tell her that Jamie Lynn was pregnant. "Noooo," she finally said softly, her voice conveying all the love, grief, and concern in the world.

Throughout the next two weeks, until the story broke in the media, I laid low, going about my business and functioning as well as I could. I got up early with my four dogs, put them out, fed them, cleaned the house, and cooked meals for me and Jamie Lynn. But I didn't want to talk to anyone, nor did I really want to leave my house at all. My friend Sherrie, who cleans my house and takes care of it when I'm away, offered to go to town to buy groceries, because I couldn't even face that small task I usually enjoy.

My part-time maintenance man, family members, friends—anyone who came by could see the grief etched on my face. Yes, grief. All I wanted to do was close the window shades and curl up on the couch, praying that I'd wake up from this unbelievable dream that our lives had become. I mourned the fact that Jamie Lynn couldn't go to her junior and senior prom, or return to traditional school, period. After *Zoey 101* ended, she had wanted to come home and be a regular teenager until she graduated, a choice I supported 100 percent. Now there would be nothing "regular" about it. My teenage daughter was going to be a mother.

Standing My Ground

Several family members, plus professionals on Jamie Lynn's management team, had come to the decision that the best thing for her would be to send her to a Christian-based residential facility in Tennessee, a kind of rehab where teen girls who are struggling with various issues, including preganancy, can go for ministry.

At first, I agreed, based on the assumption that I would be going with her and we would live together in some kind of dorm or something. I was still in shock over the news that my child was going to give birth, and I was badly rattled, fragile, uncertain; when things are not going well in my life, I tend to really question my own judgment. Add to this the fact that everybody else—including Jamie Lynn's business manager, Jamie's interventionist and AA sponsor, and Jamie himself—was saying, "This is absolutely what we need to do," and I went along with it.

When I realized that I couldn't go with Jamie Lynn, that she'd be staying there by herself, I started to come to my senses. While I admire the work they do at this facility, I couldn't see how my daughter would benefit. In fact, I thought she would be scared to death, far from home and from me. It didn't make sense to me and still doesn't. The team's thinking was that Jamie Lynn needed a break from Casey, and that she would emerge from the program stronger in her faith and more equipped to cope with the challenges of teen motherhood.

"Don't let her throw her life away on that boy," one of them said to me. But I disagreed, knowing Jamie Lynn and Casey would find their way back to each other anyway, even if we forced some kind of separation.

Jamie Lynn already had her bags packed. She thought she had no choice. But in the end I made the decision to keep her at home, close to me and to all the people who loved her and knew her.

My friend Kelly provided much-needed reinforcement. The day Jamie Lynn was supposed to leave, I called her to come over and face down the lions with me. She came immediately—brave, loyal Kelly, a farmer's wife, a Southern woman who lived light-years from Hollywood and its skewed guidelines. Kelly had to have been at least a little bit intimidated by some of the strong personalities in the room, hell-bent on sending Jamie Lynn away, but she came anyway. We commiserated behind the closed doors of my bedroom.

"Lynne, you know Jamie Lynn, and I know Jamie Lynn. None of us with these girls [she, Joy, and Margaret all had daughters Jamie Lynn's age, who had grown up together] would send one of our daughters away. She needs to be here with you and with us, people who have known her since she was little."

That's exactly what I needed to hear. As soon as Kelly left, I sat down in the living room and told Jamie and the others that I had changed my mind. "I cannot do this," I said. "This is not what she needs."

> I WAS STILL HER MOTHER, AND IT WAS UP TO ME TO PROTECT WHATEVER WAS LEFT.

To say I was raked over the coals would be like saying Louisiana is a touch muggy in July. Jamie, especially, did not mince words, yelling and ranting and accusing me of being co-dependent, among other things. But those lions could roar all they wanted to—I would not budge. When Jamie Lynn got pregnant, a door had been slammed shut, and behind it was most of her childhood. I was still her mother, and it was up to me to protect whatever was left.

Standing my ground was not easy. I'd been so passive in so many ways for so long, letting managers and agents and executives decide the paths my children would walk. Not any longer. Not while I was still their mother.

That resolution would be put to the sorest test with Britney.

twenty-seven

JERKED AROUND

Right before Britney went into Promises, after she shaved her head, I got an anonymous call from a man while I was driving in Los Angeles. "There are drugs planted in Britney's Malibu house," he said, going on to tell me that there was a conspiracy with Kevin and Britney's assistants to make my daughter look like a bad mother. I was so unnerved by the call, I missed my exit—in more ways than one.

Immediately, I called the security guards at the Malibu house and asked them to check the house for drugs. While I knew Kevin would never hurt my daughter like that, and I highly doubted her assistants would either, things were so fragile with Britney at the time that I wasn't taking any chances. She had just lost custody of the boys to Kevin, and she was at a very low ebb. It was midnight, but I turned around and drove to Britney's house and met her assistant, Allie. Along with the guards, we combed through the house, and no drugs whatsoever were to be found. Nonetheless, Allie and I were scared to death.

I didn't hear from this mysterious person again until months later. Right away, I recognized his voice. "Are you the same guy who called me

with a conspiracy theory about drugs being planted in Britney's house?"
I asked him.

"Yeah," he said. "It's me." When I told him his theory had proved
wrong, he protested: "There *were* drugs; you just didn't find them," he
said, earnestly.

I should have hung up the phone right then and there.

I didn't, and the man plunged into a proposal he had for me, to be
the spokesperson for a company he represented that wanted to sell
high-quality cubic zirconia jewelry on a home shopping network.
Again, it sounded dubious at best, but the call had come during a time
when I had been thinking and praying for a job, my own thing, where
I could go to work every day and regain some of the structure I lost
when I gave up teaching. Talking about jewelry on TV? That sounded
like fun! I actually have quite a zest for cheap jewelry, or, I should say,
beautiful jewelry that looks as if it cost a mint but is really affordable.
If you ever look at a photo of me and think I am dripping in diamonds,
don't be deceived: it's really a mixture of the real stuff and three-dollar
zirconium dioxide, bought from a Los Angeles street vendor! I was
intrigued, and I figured I had nothing to lose but a few hours if I did
meet with this guy.

I said I would meet with him, but only with an attorney present. I
called up my friend Jackie, and we decided to check it out together.

And so we met the anonymous caller, a swarthy man in his late
twenties or early thirties who appeared to be of Middle Eastern heritage.
That's the first time I laid eyes on Sam Lutfi.

Fake in More Ways Than One

He had two attorneys with him, but I could tell instantly this was not a
legitimate meeting. The man, wearing a ratty baseball hat, T-shirt, and

jeans, was sweating profusely and looked extremely nervous. It was the strangest meeting I have ever had! No one seemed to have any pitch whatsoever, including the caller, Sam, who hemmed and hawed and talked in circles, at one point pulling out some crummy-looking boxes with so-so costume jewelry inside. Finally, we just left. Obviously, nothing was going to come of this. Interestingly, during the meeting, Sam wanted to have his picture taken with me, which struck me as strange at the time, and I can't even remember if I consented. Now I know what he was up to, all right.

Awhile later, Sam called and invited Jamie Lynn, Jackie, and me to a taping of the finale of *Dancing with the Stars* with our old friend Joey Fatone, whom we knew from the days of Justin and *NSYNC, hoofing it in the finale. He excitedly told me he had an endorsement deal cooking with a shoe company, possibly for Jamie Lynn or Jackie's son, who also starred on *Zoey 101*.

"What about the jewelry deal?" I asked suspiciously.

"Oh, well, Britney put out a negative thing about you and her relationship with you online, and that kind of blew the jewelry deal out of the water."

My suspicions didn't totally subside, but he made it all sound somehow credible, reasonable. Even when the shoe deal "fell through," and we were this close to pulling the plug on this guy, he rallied just in the nick of time, inviting us to a meeting with the head of one of the top talent agencies in Hollywood. Jackie and I thought this agent would be an excellent contact for her son, Paul, a budding musician.

Jackie and I had our doubts, all right. But Sam had one more chance. If this agency executive indeed showed, then it meant Sam was legitimate. If this once again fell through, we would wash our hands of him.

The day of the meeting arrived, and, lo and behold, we got a phone call from Sam half an hour before we were set to meet. "I have a broken tooth," he explained.

Jackie was dubious, and firm: "Listen, buddy, you better just take some pain pills and come anyway," she said. "We are really going to doubt your story if this meeting doesn't happen." He balked, and we stopped answering his texts, hoping this would be the end of our association with this shifty man.

What we didn't know then was that Sam had also met Britney's then assistant, Allie, at a club, and she in turn introduced him to Britney. The two of them hit it off with Sam, and they all began to hang out together. So it was really just the beginning. He was looking for a back door, and it appeared he found one.

Svengali

Sam came into my daughter's life at a time when she was at her most vulnerable. Brokenhearted about losing custody of her precious boys, she was sad, floundering, ripe (if you ask me) for a predator to come along. If you're bleeding by the side of the road, and someone drove up and offered you a ride to the hospital, wouldn't you accept? This is the picture I have of my child during that time: defenseless and exposed, she was much more open than she ever would have been to this man, who rode in on a white horse, personable, charming, and with an air of authority, promising her he would help her get her kids back, that he would get her life back on track.

> IF YOU'RE BLEEDING BY THE SIDE OF THE ROAD, AND SOMEONE DROVE UP AND OFFERED YOU A RIDE TO THE HOSPITAL, WOULDN'T YOU ACCEPT? THIS IS THE PICTURE I HAVE OF MY CHILD DURING THAT TIME PERIOD: DEFENSELESS AND EXPOSED.

Why didn't I ride in on my own horse to help my own child? If only I could have. I felt so helpless, yearning with every cell in my body to be with her, help her, and hold her, but I wasn't able to do that. Our estrangement was so complete at that time that I couldn't even get her phone number.

Within a month or so of meeting, Sam was in complete control of her life, labeling himself her friend, her manager, her life coach. Everyone deferred to him—Britney's business manager, her record company, her lawyers—they had no choice.

He appointed himself as her gatekeeper, and there was no one he wanted to keep the gate closed to more than Britney's family. While he shut Jamie out completely, he would crack open the door a bit for me, texting me with updates on my daughter, lording over me the fact that he had complete access while I had no right of entry to my own child. But he also seemed to sense the exact moment when I was most susceptible, and he would drop his voice to a soothing, kind modulation—as if we were confidants. "I know you want to see Britney, and trust me, I am working on her. She'll let you back into her life soon." That man jerked me around like a master puppeteer.

In October of that year, I got a call I had been praying for: It was Allie. "Brit's ready to reconcile," she said. I dropped everything and caught the next flight to LA, arriving at 9 p.m., California time. As per my instructions, I met Bret, another of Brit's assistants, at the Starbucks in Malibu. Several paparazzi met us there as well, and they ended up taking us to her house, where Sam, the figurative gatekeeper, ordered the physical gatekeeper to let us in. Everyone treated him by now like a general.

Britney and I just held on to each other for the longest time. I was so happy to see her and hold her in my arms again. But in the midst of my joy, part of me wondered: was this reunion orchestrated by Sam, to help Britney get her boys back? You see, the courts looked at me as a stabilizing factor, and Sam knew that a reconciliation between Britney and me could only be a step in the right direction as far as her hopes of regaining custody. Was this a true reunion, or just another pawn in Sam's game?

Three Months Later

I had just come home with Jamie Lynn, after we went to Connecticut for a couple of weeks during Christmas to hide from the media fallout of her pregnancy. I was exhausted, physically and emotionally, and it was soothing to be back home with my dogs, sleeping in my bed, and getting my clothes out of my drawers instead of a suitcase.

One night the phone rang, and it was Sam. He was crying.

He told me Britney had been visiting with the boys, but when it was time for them to go home to Kevin's with Lonnie, their bodyguard, she locked herself and little Jayden in the bathroom. Later, I found out Sam had told Britney that Kevin had called and told her she could keep the boys longer.

I was terrified of what would happen next. I frantically called Jamie and Bryan, begging them to go see what was going on, but they had a much more blasé attitude than me, saying that Sam was blowing things out of proportion. Neither one of them would ever have anything to do with Sam, and the only reason I did was because he was the only link to my daughter, and I just *couldn't* sever it. They reminded me that Britney did not want to see any of us. "But what if she calls out for me in the crowd? I just want to be there if she needs me!" I pleaded. But the two of them were firm with a "wait and see" attitude. I can't blame them, but the whole thing was driving me frantic.

Thank God for Lonnie, the little boys' bodyguard, who called me repeatedly and assured me that Preston was just fine, asleep in the back of the SUV, and that he would not leave the premises without Jayden in his arms. Do you know how comforting that was for this mother and grandmother? Still, I was a wreck, worrying myself sick many miles from my confused, hurting daughter. If it weren't for the fact that I had to be with Jamie Lynn at that time, I would have flown to Los Angeles on the next flight.

It felt as if I were being split in two pieces as I was pulled, on one hand by the needs of my pregnant sixteen-year-old, and on the other by my twenty-six-year-old daughter, who was obviously in deep crisis; both girls seemed to need me with the same intensity. I honestly didn't know where I was supposed to be.

> THANK GOD FOR LONNIE, THE LITTLE BOYS' BODYGUARD, WHO CALLED ME REPEATEDLY AND ASSURED ME THAT PRESTON WAS JUST FINE, ASLEEP IN THE BACK OF THE SUV, AND THAT HE WOULD NOT LEAVE THE PREMISES WITHOUT JAYDEN IN HIS ARMS.

Things happened so quickly. The next thing I knew, Britney was being taken by ambulance to Cedars-Sinai Medical Center and placed under a 5150 hold, which is an involuntary psychiatric hold, for seventy-two hours. At least it was supposed to be seventy-two hours; she was actually released in twenty-four hours, at her own request. I stayed up late into the night, following my daughter's ordeal on TV and the Internet and via phone updates from Jamie and Bryan. I was horrified to see all those helicopters and fire trucks and ambulances surrounding my child's house. Why were they there? To contain one small woman, who was by then completely subdued? When I saw the photo of her in the ambulance, her beautiful brown eyes pained and haunted, something inside me broke.

What on earth was going on with my beloved child?

twenty-eight

THE GENERAL

I spent the next three weeks on my knees, in a fog of worry and confusion. All I could do was offer up prayer after prayer for Britney, wondering all the while if I should go to her, even though there was a good chance I wouldn't be allowed in the gate.

I was feeling as if my arms might as well be pulled out of their sockets. All of me longed to go be with Britney, to see if she would let me in her life and help her, but the problem was, that all of me also knew I was in the right place, right there at home with Jamie Lynn. I have never felt so cruelly divided in all of my life.

When it seemed as if Jamie Lynn had stabilized and that I could leave her in the care of a close friend, I did. I flew to Los Angeles for a four-day weekend to see my grandchildren, whom I hadn't seen in a couple of months. Of course, I hoped to see Britney with all my heart, but I wasn't really expecting to. But on the night of January 28, everything changed. I was at Kevin's, just having put the babies to bed, when I got a text from Lou: GO OVER THERE. THEY HAD A FIGHT.

Was this the breakthrough we were looking for? Sam and Britney had gotten into a terrible argument. I later learned that he called her, among other things, a "piece of trash." He said she cared more about Adnan, her current boyfriend, than her children, and that she didn't deserve to get her kids back.

> I WAS SO VERY TIRED OF
> PLAYING GAMES WITH
> SAM. *PLEASE GOD,*
> *LET THIS BE THE END.*

We didn't know it at the time but Lou, Jamie, and I had been hoping for the very same thing: we all believed the only way to loosen Sam's stranglehold on Britney was for them to turn on each other.

And we all had been praying for it. I was so very tired of playing games with Sam. *Please God, let this be the end.*

Going Inside

I jumped in the backseat of Jackie's car, and we drove as fast as we could to Britney's house. On the way, I phoned my friend Joy at home in Kentwood, asking her to pray. "You might see my tail end on TV, crawling over the fence," I said, only half-joking. I was willing to do anything to rescue my daughter.

The paparazzi were teeming outside Britney's house in Beverly Hills, but they didn't even look twice at us. They knew all the makes and models of all our family's cars, but they didn't recognize Jackie's car, and I was crouched down in the backseat. Even when a paparazzo came to the car and spoke to Jackie, between her tinted windows and the fact that I was ducking down as far as I could, with my hood pulled over my head, he couldn't see a speck of me.

"There's been a fight," Jackie told Britney's gatekeeper quietly. "I have Lynne here with me, and she wants to see how her daughter is doing."

"They are not answering right now," he said, referring, of course, to Sam, the general.

So we waited a little while.

Meanwhile, Jamie drove from the opposite end of town and arrived right at the perfect moment. "If I get in," I whispered to him, still hunkered down, on my cell phone, "you just come in after me." There were probably twenty paparazzi, swarming Jamie's truck, jumping on the car, and screaming, while there I was, hiding in plain sight, just a few feet away.

Knowing the paparazzi, they would have given up eating for a week to have known I was hiding in Jackie's car! It was so obvious to me that God was in the details, in the perfect timing of Jamie's arrival, and in concealing me so flawlessly from paparazzi eyes and cameras. It reminded me of that verse from the Psalms: "Hide me from the conspiracy of the wicked, from that noisy crowd of evildoers."

> "HIDE ME FROM THE CONSPIRACY OF THE WICKED, FROM THAT NOISY CROWD OF EVILDOERS."

Sam okayed the gatekeeper to let me in, though he never in a million years would have let Jamie in. When the gate finally swung open, there was a delay of about a minute or so, and Jamie zoomed in right after me.

Sam met Jackie, Jamie, and me at the door.

He said that Britney only wanted to see me, that she was afraid to see her dad. More like Sam was afraid. He was visibly upset to see Jamie and, believe me, the feeling was mutual.

"Her *family* is here," Jamie said, glowering. "You have to go now."

Jamie was stomping, spitting mad, but I could tell he was keeping a tight rein on his emotions. He didn't want to lose control and give Sam the chance to bring charges against him. At one point, he stalked Sam around and around the bar. "You better not be hurting my daughter," he said, over and over again, in a low, menacing voice. "Where is my daughter?"

Britney was gone, and Sam kept saying he didn't know where she was. None of us bought it for a second.

"Sam, c'mon," Jackie said, in her reasonable way. "I know you. You can track her. You can get her back here."

After about an hour, a security guard came and asked Jamie to leave. "I'm sorry," he said. "I know you're her dad, and I'm a dad too. I'm just carrying out orders."

Jamie really had no choice, leaving Jackie and me to deal with Sam and his subordinates. *We need to outsmart this guy*, I remember thinking. *We have to pretend we are not a threat.* It seemed to work: I believe Sam thought we were swallowing the idea that he was really helping Britney. Though I was afraid of him, of his hostility, cruelty, and lies, a new kind of courage kicked in that night, a God-given boldness that hadn't emerged in me until I was standing face-to-face with what I feared most: that harm would come to my child.

The General at Work

After Jamie left, two or three paparazzi came inside and made their way to the kitchen. They greeted Sam and reported Britney's whereabouts to the general. It was clear to me from the conversation that Sam had given a paparazzo one of Britney's cars to get her out of the house when he heard that Jamie and I were on our way to see Britney. Sam apparently told her that Jamie and I were coming to do an intervention.

The paparazzi seemed like his foot soldiers, his henchmen. They reported to Sam and addressed him with great respect. He instructed them to get her back to the house.

Britney came back with Adnan, who is also a paparazzo. Sam told Jackie that we needed to do whatever he tells us to do. I objected. "I'm the one who spends 24/7 with your daughter," he shot back. "I sleep in cars outside her house so she can't leave." He then said, "You people throw everyone under the bus; if you don't listen to me I'm going to make your name s—t in the papers."

The level of control he exerted was bewildering. Adnan told me that Sam hid Britney's cell phones and told her that he lost them. I believe it wholeheartedly. As I looked around the kitchen, I noticed that in the middle of the kitchen table, there was a large car battery. It was for Sam to charge his cell phone. The general told us that he threw away all of Britney's phone chargers and disabled the house phones by cutting the wires. He also disabled several of Britney's cars so she couldn't leave unattended. And how's this? Adnan told me that Sam also would hide Britney's dog, London. She would look all over the house, crying, and then Sam would bring out the dog and act like some sort of savior.

The whole scene was surreal.

Sam was visibly jealous of Adnan. He told Jackie and me to tell Adnan to leave Britney alone and to "get the f—k out of the house." Jackie refused. He then told us to tell Britney that Adnan is gay. Sam finally spoke to Adnan himself, and Adnan left.

It wasn't long before Britney came looking for Adnan. Sam told her that he was in the bathroom. "Is Adnan gay?" she asked me. Clearly Sam was playing up this angle however he could. While Britney was out of earshot, Sam told Jackie and me that we should pretend that Adnan was in the bathroom so Britney wouldn't leave.

Britney was so agitated she couldn't stop moving. She cleaned the house. She changed her clothes, many times. She also changed her three dogs' clothes several times. We talked, but it was as if she wasn't really there. She spoke in a tone and with the level of understanding of a little girl.

Britney then picked up a bottle of pills and read part of the label. "What does insomnia mean?" she asked. Sam told her that the pills will help her stay awake. Sam told Jackie and me that he grinds up Britney's pills, which were on the counter and included Risperdol and Seroquel, and puts them in her food. He said that was the reason she had been quiet for the last three days. She had been drugged and asleep. He said that her doctor was trying to get her into a sleep-induced coma so that they could then give her other drugs to treat her. I was breaking inside at every syllable he uttered about my daughter.

The Waking Nightmare

Maybe Sam could see I was distressed. He encouraged us to relax and "do tequila shots." Jackie and I protested. Britney seemed to follow our lead, but Sam kept pushing. He got out some wine and suggested that we "all do toasts." He offered us tumblers. We took the wine andand went into another room, but Britney objected and said that she wanted a nicer glass with a long stem. She had caught on to the fact that if she drank something from his hand, she could sleep for days, so she was actually stalling. Sam found a proper wine glass and poured one for Britney while our backs were turned. They then joined us in the other room, but Britney refused to drink her wine and asked to drink mine.

Shortly afterward, Sam went back into the kitchen. He stood behind a raised bar so that we could not see what his hands were doing on the counter. By then Britney had calmed down some, and Sam suggested they both go upstairs.

When they came back down a little while later, Britney was agitated again. She said she wanted to go to Rite-Aid to get lipstick. It was now past midnight, but maybe this was our chance to get her out of this madness. Jackie and I seized the chance. We would take her, we said. Sam jumped in and said he wanted to follow in his car. We told him that he shouldn't because the paparazzi were in front and would harass us. He seemed to relent, but as we were about to drive off, Sam jumped into the backseat with me. He said that when they were upstairs together, he gave

Britney something to pick up her mood. The paparazzi followed us to the store.

When we got to Rite-Aid, we all went inside, and Britney chose her lipstick. She drifted in and out of British accent the whole time. When we got to the register, Britney's card didn't work. I paid for the lipstick, and the manager told us we could leave through the side door so no one could see us. That wasn't to Sam's liking. He insisted we leave through the front door, and he wrapped his arms around Britney and me for the paparazzi to take photos. My skin crawled.

"You'd better learn that I control everything," he said. "I control Howard Grossman, Britney's business manager. I control her attorneys and the security guards at the gate. They don't listen to Britney; they listen to me." *That's why Jamie was gone tonight.* Back at the house he told me that if he weren't in the house to give Britney her medicine, she would kill herself. "If you try to get rid of me, she'll be dead, and I'll piss on her grave."

He then boasted that he had been in our family for a year and that he had done nothing but good for Britney. At one point he screamed at me.

"Sam treats me like that," Britney said, as if it were the most normal thing in the world.

It was about two or three in the morning, and Britney was meandering aimlessly around the house. She would let me hug her, but she was completely out of it. She asked about Preston and Jayden.

"When do I get to see my babies?"

"Wednesday," Sam answered.

"What do I have to do to see them?"

"Take the pills I tell you to take."

"I don't like the pills, and I don't like the psychiatrist," she protested. "Can't I see another psychiatrist so I can see my babies?"

"If I told you to take ten pills a day, you should do what I tell you to see your babies."

I was frozen by the exchange, but Jackie jumped in: "Britney, your parents can help you find a psychiatrist. The psychiatrist needs to get to know you to give you the right medicine."

Sam couldn't stand losing control of the conversation. He butted in with his voice raised. "Why don't you get back with Kevin?" he said.

"I'll do anything to get them back."

Another opportunity came around for us to steer things away from Sam.

Britney said she wanted her daddy. "I want my daddy up here. I want to talk to my daddy."

I reached Jamie on the phone and gave the phone to Britney. I heard her say that she wanted to see him.

"Right now, baby?" She said no. "Ten in the morning?"

"No, noon."

It was something.

I spent the rest of the night at Britney's house and finally got to sleep about four in the morning. For the longest time I couldn't sleep. I was so worked up, so agitated by the situation. I don't think Britney ever went to bed that night. All night long, I went through the motions of pretending I believed Sam's lies, while inside I was revolted and full of questions. How could this possibly have a good ending? It was a sense of deep shock that things had spiraled downward so fast, yet I had to control myself and not let anyone sense what I was really feeling, that my head was spinning.

The Thank-You Note

Jamie came to pick me up the next morning. Jamie gave Britney a big hug and said to her, "Baby, you're OK?"

Britney said, "I'm fine," then burst into tears.

Later the next day, on January 29, Jackie showed me a text message she had received from Sam: "Thanks for telling Jamie all your bulls—t. He just hit me. Now you guys did your deed. Much accomplished. Good job."

But he still had my daughter in his clutches. We didn't accomplish enough.

twenty-nine

BREAKING THE STRANGLEHOLD

I didn't see Britney again for two and a half days, until Wednesday night, when Sam called me and asked me to come over to the house. Since I had seen her last, I had been in a state of anguish. Clearly, this was a life-or-death situation, and I prayed without stopping for another opening. Quiet plans had been underway for six weeks for Jamie to petition the court for temporary conservatorship of Britney, but it seemed like an impossible dream at that point, with Sam still so entrenched in her life. In fact, Jamie was going to file for the conservatorship on January 22, eight days before-hand, but he and his business manager, Lou, felt God leading them to wait, fast, and pray, despite the frustration of a phalanx of lawyers.

Something drastic would have to happen for Sam to lose control and for Jamie to gain control of his daughter, who was, after all, an adult woman; I shuddered to think of what depths of desperation we would have to plumb to regain charge of our child.

When Sam called, he said he had been tipped off that somebody was coming to try to commit Britney again. "What are you talking about?" I said. "They can't take her like that!"

"Yes they can," he said, acting as if it was out of his hands. But when

I got to the house, Sam was nowhere to be found, something I thought was very odd at the time. In a flash of panic, I knew who was really behind this.

"Britney, get out of here now!" I shouted to her. "Sam wants you to be committed again! He says there are people coming to get you!" Sam showed up then and looked at me as if I had lost my mind. Poor Britney didn't know who to believe. "Come with me right now!" I begged.

Before we could act, there was a pounding knock on the door; within seconds, at least twenty police officers stormed into the house. One of them announced that they were there to apprehend Britney and take her to the UCLA Medical Center, on another 5150 hold.

"On what grounds are you taking my daughter?" I said as firmly as I could, though I was trembling.

"We have our orders," the officer practically barked at me. I was afraid to move a muscle. *Why are all these huge guys here to take my one-hundred-twenty-pound daughter?*

Britney in no way resisted them. She was polite and subdued, even as they strapped her into a gurney.

"Why do you have to strap her down like that?" I demanded. "She's not resisting you!" One of the cops glared at me. "We'll restrain *you* if you cause any problems," he said. "Just sit over there and be quiet." At this point, they had us all standing in different parts of the room, separated as if we were common criminals. I had called Jamie to let him know what was happening to Britney, and both of us were crying. How could this be happening to our daughter? She started crying for me, "Mama, Mama!" I was in agony.

"I'm here. I'm here, baby," I said, tears streaming down my face. "Please let me ride with her!" I pleaded. But they wouldn't budge. I was more afraid than when they had airlifted my comatose little boy, all those years ago.

The admittance slip of the psychiatric ward of UCLA Medical

Center said she had been driving recklessly, not taking her medicine as directed, and wasn't sleeping properly. *Aha*, I thought. *No one could know that except for Sam.* Later, I found out that he had been working in conjunction with the Smart Team, a branch of the police force that watches for DUI and reckless drivers.

Jackie; Adnan, Britney's paparazzi boyfriend; and I raced out the door after Britney as she was put into an ambulance. I could hear the whirring of helicopters circling the sky overhead, and I could see police on motorcycles and in cars, and all kinds of emergency vehicles. Afterward, I would wonder how many thousands of dollars were spent capturing one hurting, vulnerable young woman and bringing her to the hospital. It was ludicrous! We jumped in Jackie's car and followed the caravan of vehicles all the way to UCLA Medical Center, where Britney was admitted, at 4 a.m., for the second time in one month, into the psych ward of a hospital.

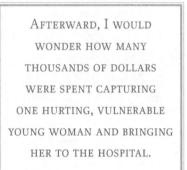

AFTERWARD, I WOULD WONDER HOW MANY THOUSANDS OF DOLLARS WERE SPENT CAPTURING ONE HURTING, VULNERABLE YOUNG WOMAN AND BRINGING HER TO THE HOSPITAL.

God's Plan Trumps Sam's

Hours passed before we were allowed to see Britney. None of the doctors would speak to any of the family members, including me—they would only talk to Sam. We knew he was there, because some of the paparazzi were texting Jackie and me, telling us that Sam had been texting them, feeding them details of Britney's condition and her surroundings in the hospital.

When we were finally allowed to visit Britney in a room, I was incensed to find Sam sitting on her bed, laughing. "What are *you* doing here?" I railed at him. "*You* put her in here!" He had a look on his face like the cat who got the cream.

"You're the one who always causes drama," he said, grinning. "They should put *you* in here."

He calmly paged a nurse, and when she got to the room, he said, gesturing to me, "Nurse, she's causing a disturbance." It was absolutely maddening. I was tearing my hair out, trying to think of a way to get this man out of my daughter's hospital room, and out of her life for good. "Just calm down, Mama," Britney said, looking at Sam for his approval.

But God had answered our prayers, and he planted a seed of doubt in the doctor's mind about Britney's gatekeeper while Sam ran out to get some food for her. Jamie and I went to the team of doctors caring for Britney and pleaded our case, telling them all I had observed at Britney's house a few nights before. The main doctor suddenly decided that he didn't have an adequate grasp on Britney's condition, or the situation as a whole; he decreed that there would be no more visitors until he could ascertain more information. When Sam sailed in about an hour later, smiling at photographers and clutching a bag of food from In-N-Out Burger, he was denied entry to Britney's room. We weren't allowed in either, but it was no small victory to have Sam barred from her side.

For three more days, Britney underwent tests and evaluation to determine what exactly was going on with her. We spent much of our time in the hospital, waiting, worrying, praying. To see my child like that—at the lowest ebb of her life—almost killed me. I was overcome with a feeling of sadness and helplessness. Britney was under the impression we had put her in there, and we told her over and over again we hadn't. I must admit, I probably never

> I MUST ADMIT, I PROBABLY NEVER WOULD HAVE HAD THE COURAGE TO COMMIT HER TO A PSYCH WARD, BUT IT ENDED UP BEING THE TURNING POINT FOR HER, AND FOR ALL OF US.

would have had the courage to commit her to a psych ward, but it ended up being the turning point for her, and for all of us.

Not only would Britney finally receive the medical care and counseling she needed, but her second committal ended up being the catalyst for driving Sam out of her life. He pulled the trigger, so to speak, setting up the whole scenario so she would be committed again, based on the belief that this would drive Adnan out of Britney's life. Sam was bitterly jealous of Adnan and knew he couldn't control him. But his plan backfired, and he was the one who ended up being driven out of her life. I kept thinking of that verse from the final chapter in Genesis: "You planned evil against me but God used those same plans for my good." That verse certainly jumps off the page for me now.

Because of all the horrible things Jackie and I saw and heard that night at Britney's house, we had the ammunition to file for a restraining order against Sam. Before my daughter was released from the hospital, a lawyer came to Jamie's apartment, where Jackie and I were asked to give an account of the events of that night. First thing Monday morning, we were in court, presenting our deposition and petitioning the judge for a restraining order against Sam and for a temporary conservatorship for Jamie. After a long day of sitting and waiting, the judge granted us both the restraining order and the conservatorship. Tears of relief and joy filled my eyes. *Thank you. Thank you. Thank you, God.* Sam was out. I could be Britney's mother again, and Jamie could be her daddy. As we walked out of the courtroom, we were taking our first steps on the road to healing our family.

thirty

A MOTHER'S HEART

We have come so far since I started putting pen to paper. After the bleakness of wintertime—literally and figuratively—my family is now experiencing the uplift we have needed for a long time.

My relationship with Britney has undergone tremendous healing. We are back to four and five phone calls a day, with her calling me about everything from Preston's potty-training progress to the darling little dress she found for her new little niece, Maddie Briann.

Maddie. Talk about an angel! That gorgeous baby was born on June 19, 2008, to a young mother who loves her more than life itself and a family eager to welcome her to our hearts. To me, she personifies grace, redemption—a fresh start. You just don't know how much you can love someone until she is snuggled up next to you, sleeping. Maddie is another glimpse of heaven to me. And Jamie Lynn is a very, very good, natural little mama. She's so independent, breast-feeding her baby and caring for her with help from Casey, but little help from the two grandmas (who are dying to get their hands on that baby!). The other day I came over when she was giving Maddie a sponge bath, and I offered to help. "I can do it, Mama," she said, as she carefully and perfectly bathed her daughter. And she can.

Full Circle

Watching my youngest child mother her own child so well brings me full circle.

My experience of motherhood has been very universal in some ways and quite unique in others. Essentially, I was the mom who taught school and cooked three meals a day and put Band-Aids on boo-boos. In my heart I am still that mom.

All my babies are grown or nearly grown now, and I have so much more knowledge and insight about the parenting process than when I began my journey thirty-one years ago with tiny Bryan. My very best days on this earth were when I had my three children at home with me, and some days I would give anything to somehow teleport back in time. I look at Bryan, Britney, and Jamie Lynn and the paths they have traveled, some of those paths anything but private. I still long for each of them to move forward in a positive direction no matter what hurdles they must over-come. It doesn't do any good to look backward at mistakes and poor choices, except to learn from them. That's just as true for me as for them.

My wish for my kids is that they make good choices, starting today if need be, to pick the high road whenever they can. And when one of them opts for the wrong route, I hope they accept the lessons that come, hold them up to the true light, and learn from them.

Watching my babies take their first steps tops most of my memories. And with each first step, they have chosen various paths—some well cho-sen and some not so well chosen. Even when they were small, I would think about what kind of journey they were on and wonder what road it would bring them down later on in life.

Regrets

Bryan and I were out for lunch one day when I told him I was going to write a book. Immediately supportive, he asked what it would be called.

"The title is *It's All My Fault*," I joked, and we both got a good laugh.

The truth is, whenever a wheel has come off with one of my children, people look for someone to blame, and often they look no farther than me, the mother. When your family is in the limelight, the public becomes your judge and jurors, and the "guilty" pronouncement has been leveled at me so many times I can't begin to count. But my biggest accuser over the years has been me.

Isn't it just like a mom to pick up the tab whenever something goes wrong with her family? I know I'm not alone in wrapping myself up in blame, time after time, as I raised my children, and even when they were grownups. I have yet to meet a mother who didn't have regrets about what she did and didn't do.

You bring these human beings into the world, these innocent little angels, and they are yours to guide for at least eighteen years, probably more. At first you are in charge, feeding them, bathing them, teaching them to keep their elbows off the table and share their toys. You balance their wants and their needs.

As they grow older, it gets so much harder. That bundle of joy starts to push and pull at your rules, challenging them every step of the way. And each child is so different. Even if you give them the same basic rules, how you lay them down and reinforce them is different for each one.

Every mother makes mistakes, though, and I'm no different. And honestly, I'd prefer to keep my regrets to myself, wouldn't you? Even if none of you ever has a child go into show business, I truly hope you can learn something from my mistakes, that as you parent your own children, something I say here might help you love and guide them with the clarity that only hindsight gives us.

Okay, here goes. Drum roll, please . . .

Building Faith. I wish I would have gone deeper with my children in terms of building up their faith. We always went to church and vacation Bible school when we were in town, but I see now that they could have benefited greatly by drawing closer to God through daily Bible reading and devotional reading. They said their prayers every night, but in retrospect, I should have helped them understand the power of prayer for every situation life throws at us. I must have felt that it would be hypocritical of me to have a huge fight with their daddy the night before, and then talk about how good the Lord is the next day. I was wrong. The Lord's mercies are "new every morning," as the Bible says. He is a redemptive God, who washes us clean whenever we ask him.

Trusting My Gut. I should not have trusted my children blindly. When I sensed something was up, I should have gone in for the kill (metaphorically speaking!), trusting my instincts and not their pleas:

- "Mama, everyone is going to that bonfire except for me!"
- "I would never do anything like that!"
- "So-and-so is allowed to do this. Why don't you trust *me*?"

In hindsight, when I suspected something was off base, I was often right. Heck, I was *always* right! I clearly remember the time Bryan was sixteen years old. He often spent the night with a friend about fifteen minutes away from our home in Louisiana. One night after football practice, he had arranged to stay the night with his friend, who was also a teammate. The boy came from a fine family, and I never had felt the need to call and check in with him while he was there. This time, though, I felt an urge to call. When I did, Bryan's friend answered the phone but was reluctant to put Bryan on the phone. "He's already in bed," the boy told me. A teenager, asleep at nine thirty on a Friday night at a friend's house? *I don't think so.* My antenna shot up, and I insisted Bryan be "dragged out of bed" and put on the phone. When my son finally picked up on the other line, I could tell immediately he had been drinking. His speech was slurred, and he wasn't making any sense. I hung up, and Jamie and I packed up the girls that minute and drove to pick him up. Turns out the boy's family had left for a few days, entrusting him to the oversight of family and close friends.

We want to believe the best in our children, but it's our job as moms to act on that sixth sense we have, the one that tells us something is not as it seems. Sometimes, my kids played me like a fiddle. I wish I had been less gullible and more suspicious—much more suspicious. My biggest mistakes in this life were from not going on my instincts, because my gut was telling me the truth.

Shelter from the Storm. When my children were young, and we were all living together as a family in Kentwood, I shouldn't have let them see me so upset about my problems. Jamie and I fought too much in front of them, and I sometimes was overwhelmed by financial matters. Though it's hard to hide your feelings when there's no gasoline for the car, I should have attempted to deal with those things behind closed doors. That's not to say it's a good idea to pretend all is well when it isn't, but I regret the extent to which my children saw me visibly upset about problems that were completely out of their control. They had enough problems growing up in an alcoholic home, and they didn't need to pile my suffering on top of theirs. Along the same lines, I wish I could have been calmer when facing issues in my marriage; parents should never argue like that in front of their children. Ideally, they should have seen Jamie and me disagree and work it out in a civilized manner. I wore my emotions on my sleeve, and my children had to pick up the pieces at times. I wish I had practiced more self-control.

Space for Myself. I wish there would have been some way to hold on to my teaching job in 2000. Britney and her manager, Larry Rudolph, begged me to quit so I could join her on tour. She was so homesick and wanted me with her as much as possible. I really wrestled with that decision—

truly, it was agonizing. In the end, did I make the wrong choice? You should never give up something that you love as much as I loved teaching. I wish I had left some space for myself, for my one passion that was mine and mine alone outside of my children. If I had kept my career, I would have something to focus on now besides my children, something positive and meaningful that would have engaged me, body, soul, and mind.

My Role as Parent. I lost control of my kids and their careers partly because I allowed professionals to unnerve me and take away my confidence. When Britney's career was exploding, I naively assumed that I should leave all the decisions to the professionals; I didn't know the music business, after all. I was a simple Southern schoolteacher. But you know what? I wish I had not lost my anchor with my kids, but instead refused to give up precious ground to people who were motivated by money, and not love. If I had gone with my gut and regarded producers, agents, managers, et al., as people to sound off on—not take their every opinion as gospel truth—who knows where we might be today?

God's Grace

I could go on. If I felt there was a purpose, I could reel off a laundry list about the ways I failed my family, from burned dinners to burned bridges. But guilt trips don't come with frequent-flier miles. At some point, a person has to file most regrets under *shoulda-coulda-woulda*, shut that filing cabinet, and throw away the key. A mother, especially, has to put her foot down and say, "No more." Shame is crippling, and in the end it serves no good purpose. I did do some things well, after all. I kept a clean, sane, orderly household despite all the craziness and uncertainty, and I provided a lot of compassion for my children, a shoulder to cry on when they most needed one.

My faith teaches me that you trade in your missteps for a salvation that is bigger than you. God takes our failures and exchanges them for release and rescue. It's called redemption.

I know God forgave me a long time ago for my blunders, and he continues to do that every day. What's harder is accepting grace from *myself.* Instead of beating a dead horse, I have to forgive myself for my shortcomings. My friends tell me one of my finer qualities is that I forgive them easily. I hope that's true.

There's nothing noble about holding on to guilt. Remember that, all you mothers reading this book who are blaming yourselves for the things you may have done wrong with your children. The truth is, we could have been *perfect* mothers, and our children may still have gone off the rails at one time or another. At some point, children are going to make their own choices, regardless of the parenting they received. It's much better to dwell on what we did well as mothers, to focus on the things that we can say with assurance we do *not* feel guilty about.

It's All My Fault? Some of it sure is, but not *all* of it—no sir! For what I am to blame for, I bring it to God and my family and ask for their forgiveness. And I try and pardon myself, let go of guilt, and walk in the freedom God provides. There's been a shift in me over the last few years, as I have gotten older and hopefully wiser. I'm not so darn worried about things, as I used to be. While I do hurt for my loved ones when they make mistakes, I don't blame myself nearly as much as I used to. Somehow I have a growing sense of peace. Like any mother, I am doing the best I can.

I know that's true for my children as well. And I hope that God gives them strength to stand, to strive, and to thrive.

Bryan

Even when Bryan was my little boy, I saw him as the kind of person who would grow up wearing suits to work. He didn't see himself that way at all, at least not until quite recently. He was always so athletic, so immersed in sports of all kinds, from the time he was a tyke. We all thought Bryan would end up in a sports career, and in fact, he finished three years of college to become a football coach. But then a broken engagement and some other difficulties made Bryan evaluate his life's direction and thus take a completely different route.

He moved to New York, leaving the safe cocoon of all he had ever known. He could have so easily stayed on the road that felt secure and predictable, but instead he faced his fears of the unknown, worked hard, and found his way. Two of Bryan's strengths are that he works well with people and has a mind for ideas and making them happen. He got into Britney's entertainment business for a while in the marketing end of things. He was the one who worked with Elizabeth Arden to broker the deal for his sister's fragrance, Curious, and he worked on many other similar projects.

He has already fulfilled some of my dreams for him. This might embarrass him, but I still see Bryan as my little soldier, having to fight for what he wants in this life. He has made some mistakes; sometimes his cart gets ahead of his horse. But patience is something I believe he will learn as he grows older. And while we're on the topic of potentially embarrassing things, I'd like to bring up the fact that Bryan needs a good woman in his life. Maybe he has already found her? He needs someone stable, with a good head on her shoulders, who will nudge him in the right direction without running the show completely, if you know what I mean. Of course, more grandchildren would be an extra bonus too! But seriously, I would love to see my son with someone who would give him a reason for all of his hard work.

Today he lives in LA and works in the movie industry on the business and production side. There he is starting to see some of his groundwork pay off. I am proud of his dedication in making his dreams come true. But, also, I admire that he took a risk years ago, at age twenty-one, with no clear picture of what the end of that new path would bring. When he ventured to that huge city, alone and far from home, he was, in a sense, searching for higher ground, seeking out a path that would not crumble the way it did when his dreams of marriage and a coaching career died.

I do wish Bryan would return to the faith of his childhood, the faith that has been my rock through this crazy, bumpy journey the whole family is on. I believe there Bryan could find the truth and peace he is looking for. Anything is possible through Christ our Savior.

What's great about Bryan is that no matter what road he's taken, he has brought along just about everyone he's ever cared about. He has a fundamental sense of loyalty that has served him well, stabilizing him on his various paths. He keeps in touch with family and friends, and has never forgotten the core unit of people who have helped him along the way. Bryan loves to play silly practical jokes on his friends, and on the other hand, he is as thoughtful a young man as you will ever meet, sending flowers to Miss Nyla and other old friends when they are sick, and thinking of others so often before himself. This faithfulness to all kinds of old friends and family members has given him a really big world to feel peaceful and safe in. The constancy of those people strengthens him as he continues to make his way.

Britney

The day after Britney shaved her head, I went out for lunch with Bryan to talk about what had happened. I'm not someone who cries in public, generally speaking, although lately that has changed a bit. That day I was devastated, broken by what had happened to my child, but I was being a mother to another one of my children. I was trying to be strong and reassuring for Bryan as we tried to sort through everything. At one point, I smiled, as if to say, "Baby, somehow, someday, it will be all right for her and for us." The tabloids must have snapped me from outside the restaurant, because the next thing I knew, there was this photo of me published in some magazines, smiling. "Lynne Spears doesn't care about her daughter," the caption read. "She doesn't have a care in the world."

If only people knew how much I cared.

Every mother reading this book probably knows that no matter what happens to your child, no matter what that child throws at you, the caring does not stop—not for a second. It is a wearisome journey to travel, although one that sometimes seems to have no light at the end of it. But in my heart of hearts, I know God is near, that he will enfold me when I am worn down and discouraged. Someone told me once that no one is immune to prayer, no one is so rich, so famous, so lost, that she is outside the power of petitioning God on her behalf.

So I move toward God and pray for fresh eyes and fresh faith to see his hope for my child.

She is not out of his reach.

Britney is my fighter. She is still that brave little girl who sang to the skies at that singing competition, years ago, after that little pinching bully tried to intimidate her.

Lord, keep her close and show her what is worth fighting for.

Britney is my sweetheart. She is still the tenderhearted daughter whose feelings were hurt so easily, and who picked up on my every mood with her uncanny, sensitive spirit.

Lord, shield her sweet soul and protect her true heart.

She was hurt when her relationship with Justin ended, but now, with years of water under the bridge, they are reuniting—for a song, anyway, a duet for one of their new albums. They have each grown in compassion and maturity; here's hoping they can be true friends and put any leftover missing puzzle pieces together for good.

Amid the ruins of fame and fortune, I still see those essential qualities inside of my child. I still see her center, her nucleus, her real "song." When she was a young girl, before the studio messed with her genuine sound, Britney sang from the depths of that truth. More than anything, I want Britney to reclaim her spiritual voice, to sing the songs of her heart that she sang when she was my "untouched" baby, before the pain and the heartbreak. When she finally salvages that voice, it should be an even sweeter and stronger song. Step by step, bar by bar, that glorious music is coming to life once again. *Thank you, God!*

Jamie Lynn

After the news broke of Jamie Lynn's pregnancy, the paparazzi and tabloid media reporters became less like pests and more like one great, big, nightmarish menace. Media minions appeared in droves by our home in Kentwood, and literally Jamie Lynn and I couldn't leave the house without fighting off a hundred or more reporters shouting questions, and cameramen shooting their flashbulbs in our faces.

It was arranged for us to go to New York City for a few days to escape that pack of snarling dogs, just licking their chops and waiting to exact their pound of flesh. While in New York, we snuck in to see a showing of the movie *Juno*, about a teenage girl dealing with a pregnancy; it had just been released in theaters. I watched that film through tears. *That poor little girl*, I kept thinking about the plucky Ellen Page character. *That poor, sweet thing. That will be my baby soon.* I was a wreck from the opening credits to the closing music. But every time I looked over at Jamie Lynn, she was completely stoic, taking it all in with her quiet, durable resolve.

She's one tough cookie, my Jamie Lynn.

When she dropped the bombshell that she was pregnant and planning to keep the baby, almost everyone in her life tried to change her mind; actually, most of her loved ones and managers wanted her to have an abortion. A plan was presented by some of her team members, that because she was so early along she could simply take a pill that would render her pregnancy a nonissue. It would be a strikingly simple solution to a huge problem, and the best part was, in their minds, no one would need to know about it—ever.

Except that Jamie Lynn would know about it—*forever*. One of her advisers took her aside and told her privately that she had had an abortion when she was sixteen, and she had regretted it ever since. That was good for her to hear, from someone she respected, a brave and truthful cautionary tale. But I am proud to say Jamie Lynn had already made up her mind and did not waver a bit, even under enormous pressure from people she looked to for guidance in this life. Her feet were put to the fire, and she stuck by her convictions with that steely will of hers.

Jamie Lynn made a mistake, one with lifelong ramifications, yet there is grace for her and Casey and little Maddie—really, for all of us. If there isn't, I'm just throwing in the towel right now! God's grace, his mercy, leniency, and kindness—that's what has met us at our place of need and transformed our mistakes—hers, mine, everyone's—into something that can glorify him.

In *Juno*, when the pregnant teen's stepmother, played by Allison Janey, had a chance to absorb the shock, she said something profound. "Someone's going to get a special blessing from Jesus in this garbage dump of a situation," she said, to her husband, Juno's daddy. That right there is a redemptive statement if I ever heard one. Sure, it's far from an ideal situation when a teenager gets pregnant, but thank God the story doesn't end there. My faith teaches me that he exchanges ashes for beauty, and that's exactly what I see when I look at my daughter, beauty—inside and out—strength, growth, and passionate purpose in her life. Jamie Lynn believes in herself and believes she can do this on her own. She is trying to detach herself from the high drama that clings to our family, and build a simple, normal life in the country, close to where she was raised, for herself, Casey, and the baby.

I respect that more than she will ever know.

The Windstorm

When fame blew through my family's existence, everything changed. I wrote earlier about the windstorm of Bryan's seizure, how that experience left us disoriented, shaken, and altered as people. We were hit by many storms over the years, including Jamie Lynn's pregnancy, but none as jarring as sudden, crazy-huge fame. In the years since 1999, I feel as if I've been surveying the damage, picking up the debris, and trying to assimilate it into the structure of my "real" life.

Years ago, when Britney's first album hit so big, I wrote this in my journal: "How do you defend this land of pretend, where there is no right or wrong?" Concerned for my daughter, I wrote more, just for her: "Take time to exhale. Really look at what you see." Clarity of vision is vital, especially in this "land of pretend" where we have found ourselves. There are so many sharks out there, people who want to be your friend and get close to you for their own purposes. Both the girls have been hurt by people who have ingratiated themselves into their lives, only to find out later that these people only wanted to look more important in the eyes of the world through their association with them. Certain religious groups, even, have preyed on them, and in my mind, their only motive was to appropriate my children and their money.

One thing I have observed is that it is hard to hold on to your core values when you have an army of people surrounding you—hair and makeup, stylists, personal trainers, and so on—who are feeding the "fame monster" with every flattering whisper.

It feels strange at first, to have everyone treat you like royalty when you come from a very down-to-earth background. The problems really begin when you start to believe these people, and a sense of entitlement begins to grow. Before you know it, you become accustomed to this new view of yourself, especially if you have no one from home around to remind you of who you are.

At times, I have been pushed to the sidelines of my children's lives, because I remind them too much of who they know they are, deep down. The people who do surround them, meanwhile, act like bumper pads, shielding them from the consequences of their behavior. Every answer is yes, and every bit of feedback is applause. These people are enablers, and the worst of the lot are dangerously manipulative. They convince whatever star it is they have attached themselves to that they are right and everyone else is wrong, including the family that loves them more than life itself. When the star is convinced, the enabler gets the cooperation and control he wants.

This is why sticking close to home and family is so important. All that you come from, all the people who don't have a thing to gain by loving you—this is what grounds a person and helps that individual know his or her own mind. I want my kids to know their own minds so very much, and they can't do that unless they know God.

My roots and my small town and my friends have always kept my feet planted on solid earth, but the single biggest grounding force in my life has been my faith. I would not have been able to survive the hurricane of fame without God's abiding strength and comfort.

Taking Control

And lately, he has toughened my hide, too, giving me the boldness to face the "enemies" that have surrounded us all in this strange life of ours. With the help of Jamie and some friends, in February 2008, we were able to root out one of the worst, most manipulative enablers who ever attached themselves to my older daughter. Though I was frightened and intimidated during that nightmarish time, I felt a core of steel within me that I can only attribute to God's work in my life, through the prayers of my friends and even strangers.

The tabloid media don't scare me as they used to; the same goes for the paparazzi. In fact, something happened recently that made me think this former pushover is becoming one hard-boiled Steel Magnolia. Or maybe I've just finally flipped my lid! I think this incident was actually a sign of progress, that I am *not* just going to lie down and take it anymore.

The Water Bottle Incident, as I have come to call it, occurred one day when I was visiting Britney in LA recently, and we decided to go to the gym for a nice workout. Well, it wasn't very nice at all, come to think of it. Britney's trainer practically killed me on that doggone spinning bike! But despite the torture of the cardio, I was having a great time, especially since Britney and I were connecting and laughing, having a wonderful mother-and-daughter time. After all she and I had been through lately, it was a balm to my soul.

When we were leaving, I immediately knew we were in trouble when someone pushed open the door to the parking garage. I heard the commotion first: dozens of paparazzi shouting and the sound of a hundred flashbulbs exploding. My heart sank. *Don't tell me we have to deal with them right now.* The scene was utter chaos, and we were instantly on guard, stressed, and wary, the peace and harmony of our time together ruined. Britney was quickly ushered to the car by her guards.

How dare they spoil my lovely time with my daughter like this!

In that moment, I kind of lost it. Something inside me just snapped.

You do not know who you're dealing with, gentlemen!

Quit.

Pushing.

Us.

Around.

Suddenly, my water bottle raised in the air, seemingly all by itself! I began squeezing that water bottle with all my might, sending off a stream of H_2O directly into the crowd of flashing cameras. Later, when I saw the footage of the incident on the internet, I could see with my own two eyes that I had this huge, Cheshire cat grin on my face. But I swear to you I don't even remember smiling. It was as if some internal switch was flipped, and I was not going to let this lunacy continue.

A paparazzo finally grabbed the water bottle out of my hand, shouting what sounded like Middle Eastern obscenities at me. He was so angry; he was trembling with rage. I actually wondered for a second if he was going to strike me. Later, I was glad Britney's guard didn't see the angry look on that man's face, or he might have attacked the man to defend me. Those guards are so protective of us all, and the last thing I would want is for him to get in trouble.

There was no real thought process to my action. If there's a fly on your shoulder, you slap at it without thinking, right? It was a protective mechanism, an automatic response, a slap at a horde of bugs. And *yeah!* it felt so good.

Bluebirds

When you are in the public eye, it seems as if people want to build you up just to see you fall. When you or someone you love fails in some way, there is a rush to judgment that would make your head spin. Accusations fly like stones, and folks line up to throw that first rock. But God is full of grace and mercy, and he is in the business of forgiveness and redemption. He picks me up, time after time, in varying stages of bruising and bleeding, and carries me.

The last three years have brought about more growth with my relationship with the Lord than ever. The combination of Sandra's sickness and death, Jamie Lynn's pregnancy, Britney's crises, and the efforts to connect with her and my grandchildren has sometimes felt overwhelming. I have been brought to my knees again and again, where really all you can do is pray.

When I'm on overload, I go into a zone of my own. I pull away from everyone. I can't even eat; all I can do is clean like crazy and pray, pray, pray. I can't even talk during times like this—all I do is cry. Sometimes, my body breaks down, and I catch some kind of flu or virus. It sounds extreme, but sometimes it is the only way for the Lord to get my undivided attention. When I'm broken like that, physically and emotionally, I can hear his voice clearer. He speaks to me in so many ways.

One time a white rosebud appeared in my flower garden, and there were no roses of any color planted on my entire property. Another time, when I felt particularly low, I was sitting in my garden when a bluebird came and perched near me as I drank my coffee. He lingered so long, it felt as though I had a visitor.

God has brought thunder and lightning and rain when I needed to stay in and feel protected from my own storms of life.

Every day, I read a daily devotional with a story and a Scripture passage. I can't even count the number of times the story or the passage has applied perfectly to whatever I am going through at the moment.

When I reflect, I realize something: the fame that came crashing into my life may have been a shock to me, but God was not surprised. Everything that has happened to my family has passed through his hands. It says in Scripture that God chastens those he loves, and through that chastening we emerge stronger and closer to him. He must really love me.

SANDRA'S LEGACY

☙

*When a good or great person's life comes to its final
sunset, the skies are illuminated until long after he is out
of view. Such a person does not die from this world,
for when he departs he leaves much of himself
behind—and being dead he still speaks.*

—HENRY WARD BEECHER,
FROM A JOURNAL ENTRY I WROTE
SOON AFTER SANDRA DIED

The only promises we have in this life are from God, that he'll walk with us, comfort us, and that everything that passes through our lives first passes through his hands. One of the entries from my poetry journal talks about the fact that we can't see into the future, or for that matter, glimpse the clear skies above the clouds. "In life, we must not know / If the path were easy, one could not grow." I wrote, by then having my share of trials and grief, but still blissfully unaware that I would one day lose the mainstay of my whole life, my beloved sister, Sandra. Had I known that the future would bring a loss full of anguish, would I have hardened my heart to the blessings of every minute spent with her? Maybe so. Probably so. And there were so very many blessings I might have missed out on.

My sister's legacy is massive, and how could I better live in that heritage than to train myself to be more like her? I fall short of Sandra in so many ways, but I do try. These days, when there is a problem thrown at me, I, too, try to think a long time before I say or do anything. And I'm trying to get my mind off my own problems and think about other people more, just as Sandra always did. It's biblical, the way she lived. When you get off your own stuff and focus on others, your own lot in life doesn't feel so bad.

As I write these words, it's been almost one year exactly since we lost Sandra. Missing her seems to come in waves. Anyone who has lost a loved one can relate to that feeling of being sort of okay about your loss, accepting it in a way, and then *bam!* Another wave of grief threatens to pull you undertow.

Like most people in mourning, I have regrets about time not spent with Sandra. I wish I had stayed in Kentwood the November before she died and spent every hour I could with her. Deep down, I think I knew she was really near the end, but after Thanksgiving I returned to LA with Jamie Lynn so she could tape *Zoey 101*. Again, I was in denial— or was it that I refused to give up? Another part of me said she had more time. I would give anything to have that month back with my sister, but it's gone. My heart aches every day as I come to terms with that decision.

If you've lost someone dear to you, someone irreplaceable and unspeakably precious, you understand why I still wear my sister's bathrobe in an attempt to wrap myself up in her, to have some tangible remembrance of her warmth, her vitality, her presence. She was *real*. She was here once and that ratty bathrobe proves it! You get it, don't you?

My prayer for me and for you is that we find healing for this journey we never, ever wanted to take. God holds you and he holds me in his strong hands, healing every wound in his time and place. The hard hours and days and weeks will not overwhelm us. And as difficult as it is to believe some days, I cling to the truth that there are great times ahead, even after tremendous loss, even after losing my inseparable other half.

Some mornings I just want to wake up and call my sister. We loved springtime best. Sandra and I would sit in the garden and have a lunch of tuna, crackers, and cheese, and of course, sweet tea. We'd talk about her flowers and my flowers and our families and how everybody's garden was doing. This year her garden is especially beautiful and full. Laura Lynne has kept up her mama's flowers so well; she is so much more to me than just a niece. Laura Lynne has become in some ways the touchstone in my life that her mother always was to me.

Every time I see some gorgeous flowers, I want to call Sandra and tell her about them, which makes me think about what she's doing in heaven. I picture Sandra and Mama, sitting on a porch swing, drinking sweet tea and talking about me. I think they are often shaking their heads and laughing, like, "Wonder what Lynne's up to now?"

Right before she died, Sandra was talking about her next home and what it might be like. She said she'd know right when Kathy and I got to heaven because she'd be able to hear Kathy's loud voice right away. She'd know exactly where that big mouth was coming from! "And Lynne," she said. "I'll know you're coming because you'll be talking on your doggone cell phone, and then all chaos will break loose in heaven." Sandra said if she heard a cell phone ring in heaven, she knew I'd be there somewhere!

Some days, when I am missing her so much it feels like a physical pain, I can hardly wait to dial her number and have her pick up and say, "Hey, Lynne!"

That will be a glorious day.

One More Gift

Three months after Sandra died, on Jamie Lynn's sixteenth birthday, we received an astounding gift. Actually, this gift felt like a special delivery from the great beyond. Even though Sandra was now a resident of heaven, before she died she had planned one last present for Jamie Lynn, the sixteenth collectible doll in a series of dolls Sandra had been giving Jamie Lynn every year on her birthday. Her best friend in the world, Kathy, made sure Jamie Lynn got that doll on the right day. The doll came with a card, signed by Sandra herself.

I don't have to tell you that even though Jamie Lynn outgrew dolls a long time ago, neither she nor any of us will ever outgrow that doll. It will always hold pride of place.

Years from now, that gift will age and get dilapidated—just like the rest of us—but the memory of the giver won't. It will shine, reminding us of the mother, aunt, and sister who wanted nothing from us and everything for us.

To me, that doll seemed to carry with it a message that even though Sandra had left this earth, she was still somehow taking care of us all, just one more time.

acknowledgments

FROM LYNNE SPEARS

Many thanks to the wonderful people who have not only enriched my life, but offered encouragement and support through its many chapters:

Sandra, my cherished sister, who was the primary inspiration for this book; and Reggie, who has been not only a brother-in-law but my surrogate father.

My beautiful children, God's gift that fulfills my life: without you, I would not know what real love is. I thank the Lord every day for sharing you with me.

Laura Lynne, my treasured niece: we've always been so close, but now we have become even closer. You are my third daughter.

My brother, Sonny, and his beautiful family: Wanda, Kevin, Blake, Brittany, Barrett, and Blaine. I find comfort in my steadfast family. You share my childhood memories. You are the constant in my life.

Thank you, Jamie, for some of the best memories of my life. Together we have three beautiful children that I will always love unconditionally. Regardless of our differences, we will always be family.

Agknowledgments

My old friends: Jill, Joy, Kelly, Margaret, and Sherrie. You are my friends, my confidantes, my strength. Thank you for always being there and listening to me. You are my counselors and my lifelines.

To my God-given new friends, Jacki and Kathy: you walked with me through the worst fires in my life. We prayed, we devised master plans, and we even found humor in the worst of times.

To Lorilee Craker, the beautiful spirit who took all of my thoughts and emotions, and organized them so that, together, we could create this story that best defines my life;: you understand who I am. God brought us together, and I believe I could not have written this book with anyone but you.

My community of friends, the many names I may not have mentioned, but who are indeed loved—you know who you are: thank you for the support, encouragement, and prayers that only come from "homefolk."

To the late Mark Steverson: a brilliant man and good friend of the family, who first encouraged me and started my wheels turning to write this book years ago.

To Lou Taylor: thank you for believing I had a story to tell and for the faithfulness in making it happen. It is a blessing to see that God uses all things for the good of those who love him.

To David Dunham: you were for me and believed in me from the start, and now we have this beautiful book, my gift to my children.

To Joel Miller: everyone should have the kind of experience I have had with you as my publisher. You and Kristen Parrish have given this book the skillful guidance that only could have come from the two of you. I appreciate you both very much.

To Mike Hyatt: "thank you" seems too small a sentiment. You truly believe in redemption and in the fact that our Lord does create "beauty from ashes." I appreciate that, despite the twists and turns over this past year, your belief in this book never diminished.

To Chip MacGregor and Miller Hogan: for making sure all my i's were dotted and my t's were crossed.

From Lorilee Craker

My abundant gratitude and a latte to the following: Chip Macgregor and Lou Taylor for bringing me this project. Erika Pott, MD, and fellow hockey mom, for the medical input. The great and mighty Guild—Ann Byle, Tracy Groot, Shelly Beach, Alison Hodgson, Cynthia Beach, Sharon Carrns, Angela Blyker, and Katrina De Man, for laughs (and tears), bountiful support, and of course that emergency gift card to San Chez! Other pals who listened and remained calm: Twila Bennett, Pastor Joy Bonnema, Torey Prinsen, Becky Wertz Walker, and Nancy Rubin. To Linda Van Steinvoorn for dropping everything to watch my kids. Ditto to Sheri Rodriguez—"Shay-Rod"—who dropped everything *and* bolstered me time and again. To Pastor David Beelen at Madison Square Church, who, true to form, understood this project's worth immediately, and who gets the concept of grace and redemption; and Judy King, for prayer and wisdom.

To John Gonzalez and Betsy Musolf at the Grand Rapids Press, for your support, discretion, and great flexibility.

To Kristen Parrish, a lovely person and a talented editor, and Joel Miller, for suggesting mustard greens and for making me bring my A game. You need to embrace hockey, but other than that, you're a sapient dude! To Mike Hyatt, for standing firmly behind this book from Day One, no matter what happened along the way.

Julie Barnhill: for being my unpaid, unofficial life coach, and for your strength, courage, and wisdom.

To my mom, Linda Reimer, for love, support, and prayers.

To my husband Doyle as un-Hollywood as a person can get, who understood from the start that people are just people. Your unwavering support and love are a boon to my life. And to my beautiful children, Jonah, Ezra, and Phoebe, for sharing Mom and for being such cool kids. I am proud to be your mother.

And finally to Lynne Spears, many thanks for being so great to work with, and for introducing this Northern woman to your wonderful friends and family (Joy, thanks for the note and the . . . well . . . you know!), as well as to the best sweet tea ever and a crawfish boil in Mississippi. It means much that you trusted me with your stories and your heart. I knew within half an hour that you were not the woman I had read about, and that impression only grew stronger as time went on. I am proud to tell your incredible story of redemption and grace to the world.

about the authors

LYNNE IRENE BRIDGES SPEARS was born in 1955 in Magnolia, Mississippi. She is the youngest of three siblings and grew up in Kentwood, Indiana. She has a degree in elementary education from Southeastern Louisiana University. She and her ex-husband, Jamie, have three children, Bryan James, Britney Jean, and Jamie Lynn. Lynne is the coauthor with her daughter Britney of the 2001 novel, *A Mother's Gift* that was later made into a movie for Lifetime Television.

LORILEE CRAKER, a native of Winnipeg, Manitoba, now resides in Grand Rapids, MI, where she proudly drives a minivan to hockey, gymnastics, and everywhere in between. The author of ten books, including *Date Night in a Minivan: Revving Up Your Marriage After the Kids Arrive*, and *A is for Atticus: Baby Names from Great Books*, Lorilee moonlights as an entertainment reporter for *The Grand Rapids Press*. She and her husband Doyle have three children, Jonah, Ezra, and Phoebe.